HOW TO MAKE
TEA

HOW TO MAKE
TEA

THE SCIENCE BEHIND THE LEAF

BRIAN R. KEATING
& KIM LONG

ABRAMS IMAGE, NEW YORK

Editor: Sarah Massey
Designer: Ginny Zeal
Production Manager: Kathleen Gaffney

Library of Congress Control Number:
2014959319

ISBN: 978-1-4197-1797-0

Copyright © 2015 The Ivy Press Ltd

This book was conceived,
designed, and produced by
Ivy Press
210 High Street
Lewes, East Sussex
BN7 2NS, UK

Publisher: Susan Kelly
Creative Director: Michael Whitehead
Editorial Director: Tom Kitch
Art Director: James Lawrence
Commissioning Editor: Stephanie Horner
Editor: Kate Duffy
Design & Graphics: Ginny Zeal
Illustrator: John Woodcock

Printed and bound in China

Color origination by Ivy Press Reprographics

10 9 8 7 6 5 4 3 2 1

THE ART OF BOOKS SINCE 1949

115 West 18th Street
New York, NY 10011
www.abramsbooks.com

CONTENTS

INTRODUCTION

This book is a concise guide about how to optimize the tea experience and turn tea leaves and hot water into a remarkable beverage. Beginning with a brief history of tea, the book continues with an examination of tea chemistry, and a guide to the terminology that will help you when buying tea. Tea-brewing techniques and tools are unveiled alongside the science behind brewing every major style of tea, as well as acknowledging its significance among diverse world cultures. Brewing good tea is easy; brewing perfectly splendid tea simply requires a little extra knowledge and preparation.

The origins of tea as a beverage reflect more than 5,000 years of complex, colorful, and global history. Tea germinated in ancient China and then spread into Japan, India, and eventually the western hemisphere. The story spans legendary Chinese emperors and Japanese monks who revered tea for its uplifting properties, and on to the emboldened British entrepreneurs who commercialized tea production in India during the 1800s. Tea has been traded, brewed, and prized worldwide ever since.

Every tea-producing geographic origin generated a series of unique post-harvest processing methods, independently giving character and cultural nuances to the taste, color, and aroma imparted by its native tea plants. An estimated 2,000 unique tea styles now grace the planet; different leaf shapes, sizes, and oxidation levels during processing are chief among the differing characteristics. Yet all tea types, whether black, oolong, green, or white, come from the same genus and species of plant, *Camellia sinensis*.

According to the Tea Association of the USA, tea is now the second most popular beverage in the world (after water) and a closer examination reveals why this has occurred. The tea plant is a virtual storehouse of natural compounds scientifically documented to support human health and well-being: plentiful antioxidants, amino acids, proteins, minerals, vitamins, and other constituents feed the body and brain. Like its sister beverage coffee, some of tea's traditional appeal comes from its caffeine content, but the similarities end there. The caffeine content of tea is a central nervous system stimulant, optimizing mental alertness and physical reaction times, yet a fascinating amino acid found in tea—L-theanine—exerts a calming effect. This curious set of opposites—yin and yang, in Chinese philosophy—may explain why so many people consider their tea breaks refreshing and uplifting, as well as soothing and relaxing. From its origins thousands of years ago in a remote part of the globe, to its emergence as a major commodity in world trade, tea is surging forward once again as a healthy, functional, and enthusiastically embraced beverage.

The Tea Plant

A BRIEF HISTORY OF TEA

The history of tea intertwines mythology, fact, legend, and cultural folklore. This story starts inside ancient forests and temples, and transitions to a prominent place within modern, global commerce through an amazing patchwork of interconnected events. Trying to unravel this colorful tea lineage involves both detective work and botanical archaeology.

Of the three major beverages served hot—coffee, tea, and cocoa—tea is number one in the world. According to the latest statistics, about 66 billion gallons (300 billion liters) of commercial beverages are consumed worldwide annually; of this total, more than 21 percent are hot teas, by far the leading category.[1]

Tea plants in recorded history can be traced to ancient China, circa 2737 BCE, noted then by Emperor Shen Nung, who was also a legendary herbalist. One story relates that when Shen Nung became ill while testing various herbal concoctions, some leaves from a wild tea plant fell into one of his mixtures. As a possible remedy, he drank some of the tea-infused liquid and felt much better. He named the tea plant *cha* in Mandarin Chinese.

No written references to tea appear in Chinese literature for another two millennia. Between 1122 BCE and 22 CE, tea once again surfaced in published records; the first tea-drinking accessories date from this era as well. Competing lore has it that tea culture originated within India and followed the spread of Buddhism into China, Japan, and elsewhere in Asia. However, there is no solid evidence that Prince Siddhartha Gautama—the founder of ancient Buddhism—ever traveled to China. Regardless, both China and India, and possibly Burma (Myanmar) and Thailand, are within the native home range of wild tea plants. Although the plant may have been widely used as an herbal medicine, the Chinese were the first culture to use it as a beverage.

[1] World consumption of beverages, Wageningen Academic Publishers.

THE ORIGINS OF TEA

In the eighth century, Buddhist monks reportedly introduced tea in compressed "cakes" from China into Japan, spawning the Japanese tea culture. These tea cakes were used to create the earliest forms of Japanese-style matcha tea. In 780 CE, Chinese writer Lu Yu published the first treatise on tea: *The Classic of Tea*. In the 1100s, the first Japanese tea farms started using seeds from Chinese tea plants. During this time, various forms of "cake tea" were utilized to make matcha; one would break off a small piece from a tea cake, crush it into a powder, and then whisk it with hot water into a frothy brew.

During the Ming Dynasty (1368–1644 CE), infused leaf-style tea preparation became somewhat common in China. Most of the tea consumed in all of Asia up to this point was green tea; in the late 1500s, black tea processing commenced in Fujian Province (China).

An early Japanese tea ceremony; these events focus on aesthetics and ritual.

EAST MEETS WEST

By the early 1600s, Dutch and British traders began shipping Chinese tea back to Europe and Great Britain. During this germinal period, characterized by the energized expansion of the emerging global tea trade, the legendary East India Company started transporting Chinese black teas to England, fueling a relentless and growing thirst for this "black gold," also popularly referred to as "bohea tea." Tea swept through much of Europe during the 1600s, especially France and Holland. The fledgling East Coast colony of British North America began brewing tea in the early 1650s from imported supplies.

In 1773, the East Indies Company procured a monopoly on the sale of tea to all British colonies through an act of Parliament, an act that also imposed a new tea tax upon the American colonies. The outcome was the Boston Tea Party on December 16, 1773, when a group of colonists dressed as Native Americans threw tea from British ships into Boston Harbor to protest against the taxation. Less well-known are nine other "tea parties" that occurred shortly thereafter in other harbors along the eastern coast. These events culminated in the American Revolutionary War and helped establish a coffee-drinking culture in the country, a habit that has dominated hot beverage consumption into the early twenty-first century.

By the mid-1800s nearly 5 percent of the entire British economy revolved around tea commerce. Political strife between China and the British government ended the monopoly that the East India Company had on the tea trade, but also triggered zealous British tea professionals to seek out new sources of tea.

Attempts by the British at seeding tea fields within India commenced in 1788, largely unsuccessfully. From the mid-1800s, tea commerce was focused upon establishing viable agricultural operations elsewhere as well, including Japan, Taiwan, and Ceylon (now Sri Lanka), even as tea produced in China was sped across the globe in clipper ships, the fast sailing vessels developed just for this purpose.

Tea is thrown overboard during the Boston Tea Party, 1773.

In spite of its energized tea commerce, British officials knew they needed more firsthand information about the tea industry as it had been perfected for thousands of years within China, from basic agricultural practices to the botany of the plants themselves. In 1835, Darjeeling (in Northeast India) was annexed, paving the way for the large tea plantations that followed a few decades later. In 1848, Scotsman Robert Fortune was engaged to gather everything possible about Chinese tea production and to smuggle live tea plants—seeds and seedlings—out of China and into India. The mission was full of intrigue, danger, and violence. This exceptionally successful act of industrial espionage and the politics behind it were instrumental forces that triggered the Opium War in China in 1839. This was a rebellious reaction in China to British attempts to offset the trade imbalance—in China's favor—between the two countries, largely triggered by heavy imports of Chinese tea into England.

Over ensuing decades, the British Empire was eventually able to import more tea from its colonies than from China, and tea production inside Japan, Ceylon, and other nations rose dramatically. Tea began to be traded and sold globally with new supply channels and a much greater variety of teas.

TEA IN THE UNITED STATES

The first widely-known packaged tea brand in the United States was Thea-Nectar, a product of the Great Atlantic & Pacific Tea Company in the mid-1800s—still in business as A&P. Advertisements for the product proclaimed "Thea-Nectar is a pure black tea with the Green Tea flavor." Though tea was a major part of the birth and expansion of A&P, its rapid growth resulted as much from the development of a chain of grocery stores across the country. Thomas Lipton, who in 1890 established large tea plantations in Ceylon, was even more instrumental in making packaged tea a widespread household commodity. The company bearing his name was launched in 1893, in Hoboken, New Jersey, and by 1898, his products were sold throughout the world. Wide availability through an emerging network of grocery stores helped fuel this product's recognition.

The twentieth century spawned most of the modern retail concepts now familiar to consumers, including shopping malls, fast-food franchises, and supermarkets. Tea was carried along in this wave as a commodity that benefited from mass-market packaging, convenience, and affordability, all established in the late 1800s, but not in full stride until the 1900s. By the end of the twentieth century, American tea drinkers began to embrace exotic new flavors, improved packaging (ready-to-drink bottled tea), and teas made from organic leaves. The era of specialty tea began to accelerate.

ICED TEA IN AMERICA

Tea chilled with ice was drunk in the Deep South at least as early as the 1870s, though at the time it was mostly made with green tea. Iced tea, credited as an American invention, was a treat largely enjoyed only by wealthy Southerners; ice harvested, stored, and shipped in from Northern states made this possible. Sweet tea, a commonplace Southern staple, dates from this period.

THE MANY NAMES OF TEA

Carolus Linnaeus, the renowned Swedish botanist, is credited as the originator of the system of scientific nomenclature for tea. **In 1735, he published his pioneering work, *Systema Naturae*, assigning the term *Camellia* to a group of flowering plants from Asia, although this group did not include tea in his original scheme.**

Camellia was coined to honor Georg Kamel, a Jesuit priest and missionary in the Philippines, whose chosen name in Latin was *Camellus*. Linnaeus honored Camellus after his death in 1706, because of Kamel's contributions to research on Asian botany, altering the term and transferring the title to the genus. This honor was bestowed although there was no evidence that Kamel himself was familiar with any of the camellias. Most modern usage of the term favors the pronunciation "ca-meel-ia" though the correct form should be "ca-mell-ia."

Linnaeus named the tea plant with its first formal term, *Thea sinensis*. He knew of the plant from Dutch traders, who imported tea from Java, introducing it to most of Europe (Russian and Portuguese traders were also pioneers in this early phase of commerce). The Dutch called it *te*, repeating what they heard it called at its source. Linnaeus doubled up on this term with the recognition that the word could also refer to Theia, a Greek goddess who was the mother of Helios (the Sun), Eos (the Dawn), and Selene (the Moon). Theia was revered as the goddess of light, imparting special emphasis to this Asian import.

In advance of Linnaeus, Engelbert Kaempfer, a German scholar, encountered tea on explorations in India and Japan, and also used the term *thea* as early as 1712. *Sinensis* is the Latinized word for "from China." To designate species, some botanists of the era opted for *Thea viridis* and *Thea bohea*, as many believed that the two distinctive types of processed tea—green and black—must come from different species of the tea plant. *Viridis* was Latin for "green" and *bohea* a transliterated form of the Chinese word *wu-i*, referring to the hills where the tea originated. *Thea bohea*, or bohea tea, is what we think of today as black tea. There is no connection to Bohemia, the region in Eastern Europe, where the term had a different origin; there it came from *bohème*, the French word for gypsy. As tea entered English culture, it was first pronounced "tay," still used in some dialects today.

The original botanical term coined by Linnaeus did not survive long. In 1818, the genus was redubbed *Camellia*, and the tea plant officially became *Camellia thea*. In 1905, the International Code of Botanical Nomenclature declared that the tea plant was a single genus and species, fixing the official term as *Camellia sinensis (Linnaeus) O. Kuntze*. This refers to Otto Kuntze, a German botanist, who in 1887 placed the tea plant within the *Camellia* genus originally designated by Linnaeus.

TEA NAMES AROUND THE WORLD

Afrikaans	tee	Hindi	chai	Romanian	ceai
Arabic	shai	Hungarian	tea	Russian	chay
Bengali	cā	Icelandic	te	Serbian	čaj
Burmese	laathpaatrai	Indonesian	teh	Sinhala	tae
Czech	čaj	Irish	tae	Slovak	čaj
Chinese Amoy	te	Italian	tè	Somali	shaaha
		Japanese	o-cha	Sudanese	téh
Chinese Cantonese	cha	Javanese	teh	Spanish	te
		Korean	cha	Swahili	chai
Chinese Mandarin	ch'a	Latin Modern	thea	Swedish	te
Danish	te			Tamil	tēnīr
		Latvian	tēja	Thai	chā
Dutch	thee	Malay	teh	Turkish	chay
Esperanto	teo	Nepalese	ciyā	Urdu	chā
Filipino	tsaa	Norwegian	te	Vietnamese	trà
Finnish	tee	Persian	chā	Welsh	te
French	thé	Polish	podwieczorek	Yiddish	tyy
German	tee	Portuguese	cha	Yoruba	tii
Greek	tsái	Punjabi	cāha	Zulu	itiye
Hebrew	teh				

THE BOTANY OF TEA

The leaves that produce tea come from a bushy plant native to Asia, as already mentioned, the plant genus *Camellia*. This genus includes about 250 different species, all originating in East Asia. In the modern world, camellias are better known for their ornamental flowers (*C. japonica*) than as the source for the beverage known as tea.

A single species of the genus *Camellia*—*Camellia sinensis* (L.)—yields all of the tea grown for commerce around the world. The tea plant is a woody perennial and in one of its wild forms can grow 30 to 50 feet (9 to 15 m) in height. Lu Yu, who wrote *The Classic of Tea*, described tea trees so large that they had to be felled, in order to harvest the leaves. In Yunnan, China, there reportedly exist ancient tea trees dating back more than 3,000 years. However old they may be, most of these ancient tea trees reside in protected forests and, amazingly, their leaves are still harvested and processed into "made tea" (the term for post-harvest tea suitable for brewing), in a process controlled by government permits.

TEA VARIETALS

Two main varieties of the tea plant account for all processed tea. The main Chinese tea plant is *Camellia sinensis sinensis* (China bush); the other is *Camellia sinensis assamica* (Assam or India bush), a native of Northeast India. The Chinese variety is shorter and bushier; the Assam variety is more tree-like, at least in the wild. Some experts believe that there is also a third variety of the tea plant, *Camellia sinensis cambodiensis* (Java bush), a question not yet formally settled in the botanic community. The long-running practice of intentional and unintentional crossbreeding makes it increasingly difficult to identify any individual variety as a pure type; modern DNA science is being used to refine this quest. Although some wild tea plants have been identified, and even protected under governmental mandates, they are largely off-limits in non-cultivated forests in India and China.

The tea plant has simple (single) leaves that are oval to lance-like in shape, dark green in color with a glossy surface, finely serrated around the margins, and alternate in placement along the stems. Leaves from different varieties of tea plants can vary in thickness according to the altitude where they grow; in general, the higher the altitude, the thinner the leaf. In terms of the quality of the final product, thinner leaves yield higher quality teas.

Tea plants produce small, white flowers with yellow stamens that look like smaller versions of their popular cousins, the ornamental camellias. Like the ornamentals, these flowers have a subtle, pleasant scent and appear as single units or in small, even-numbered clusters. The flowers are important to tea plants, as *Camellia sinensis* requires an outside pollinator in order to reproduce; bees and other insects provide this service. Seeds are produced within small, hard fruits that are green to brown in color, and contain one to four seeds per capsule.

**CAMELLIA SINENSIS
VAR. SINENSIS**

**CAMELLIA SINENSIS
VAR. ASSAMICA**

A hardy evergreen shrub or small tree, *Camellia sinensis* var. *sinensis* has leaves that are small and narrow. It will grow to 10 feet (3 m) left to its own devices, but in plantations, it is usually trimmed to the height of a picker's waist.

A variety of the Chinese species, *Camellia sinensis* var. *assamica* has leaves that are larger than the Chinese variety. It is indigenous to Assam, and is the source of most Indian black teas.

PARTS OF THE TEA PLANT

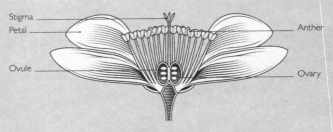

Stigma

Petal

Ovule

Anther

Ovary

FLOWER

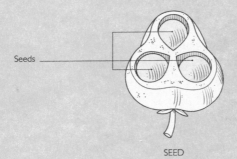

Seeds

SEED

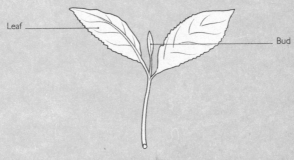

Leaf

Bud

LEAFSET

THE LEAFSET

The parts of the tea plant that are most desirable for the teapot are the two small new leaves at the end of a stem and the bud of an emerging leaf, together called the "leafset." The leaf bud alone is selected for use in white teas. Because tea, like most plants, concentrates more nutrients, volatile oils, and chlorophyll in emerging leaves, buds, and leafsets, spring harvests produce the most coveted teas, as these vital constituents are also instrumental in generating flavor. As a perennial, a tea plant can produce new growth throughout the year; and the plant itself can live for decades, even well beyond 100 years. The Chinese varieties that grow at higher altitudes produce new growth four to five times a year; Assam varieties at lower altitudes actively produce growth as often as every ten days. However, some of the highest quality teas, for example, special Chinese green teas called "Qing Ming," are harvested only once a year, within a two-week period in the early spring. Traditionally, a tea harvest is called a "flush" and the first flush produces the highest quality.

Beyond creating the flavors, aromas, and colors unique to tea, certain compounds found in the plant occur for two other vital reasons: to provide nutrition for promoting growth and to protect against attack from insects. Sugars—produced by chlorophyll and other substances— fatty acids, and amino acids in *Camellia sinensis* trigger and sustain the growth of new leaves. These compounds also contribute to the complexities of aroma and taste in brewed tea. Caffeine and polyphenols serve to deter plant-eating insects, and they are also more concentrated in new leaves, because with sugars concentrated at these sites, they are prime targets for insects.

GROWING CONDITIONS

The tea plant favors cool, humid tropical highlands, such as those found in its home range in Asia. Some sources narrow its origins to the source of the Irrawaddy River in Southwest China near its border with Myanmar. Growing zones range from "warm temperate dry" to "tropical very dry" to "moist forest life" with precipitation ranging from 25 to 120 inches (63 to 300 cm) and annual temperature ranges from 60 to 80°F (16 to 27°C). *Camellia sinensis* is slow-growing, preferring soil that is slightly acidic, but different varieties are adapted for a range of growing conditions, including toleration of frost, or for lower or higher altitudes. In China, some of the most favored teas grow in the mountains, and the highest-quality varieties are carefully tended in partial shade. In general, altitudes above 4,000 feet (1,220 m) are associated with the most notable teas, with 6,000 feet (1,830 m) considered optimum. Assam varieties typically grow at lower altitudes, but some are cultivated as high as 6,500 feet (1,980 m).

CULTIVARS

From the two main varieties of tea plant, *sinensis* and *assamica*, planters have produced many different cultivars: these are the equivalent of breeds in animals. Tea plants are easily cross-pollinated. They freely interbreed to produce plants exhibiting select attributes of the respective partners. Cloning, the process of creating exact copies of an organism (in plants, often done through leaf cutting and grafting), is increasingly used to maintain consistency in cultivars, reducing unwanted effects from natural, uncontrolled hybridization. Clones are increasingly important as tea production expands into new areas that pose risks to commercial production—less than optimal growing conditions such as too much or too little climatic moisture—and to generate characteristics intended for the rapidly increasing health-oriented consumer market—higher concentrations of beneficial, antioxidant catechins is one such target.

CLASSIFICATION OF TEA

Kingdom
Plantae (plants)

Division
Tracheophyta (vascular plants)

Subdivision
Spermatophytina (seed plants)

Class
Magnoliopsida

Order
Ericales

Family
Theaceae

Genus
Camellia

Species
Camellia sinensis

Other desirable objectives sought from tea plant cloning are optimizing the expression of compounds that affect aroma and flavor, especially polyphenols and amino acids. Commercial varieties of the tea plant are available by the thousands, with names such as *Benifuuki*, *Yabukita*, and *Da Bai*, some of them in use for hundreds of years. There are over a thousand subvarieties of the *Camellia sinensis* plant.

Sometimes, the seeds of the tea plant are harvested to produce tea oil, a product that shares many of the healthy components of tea itself. Tea oil should not be confused with tea tree oil, however. The tea tree (*Melaleuca alternifolia*), a native of Australia, is not related botanically to *Camellia sinensis*. Another member of the *Camellia* order, however, does yield beneficial oil. *Camellia oleifera* is also called the tea oil plant or oil-seed camellia, and like all members of this genus, originates in Asia. This oil is used for cooking throughout China, as an ingredient in skincare products, and as an anticorrosive coating for tools.

TEA GROWING IN AMERICA

Tea does grow and thrive in America; the first known attempt was in 1799 in South Carolina. Attempts to create commercial tea-growing operations, as far west as Texas, all failed, mostly because of the intensive manual labor required for harvest. There are a few small commercial tea-growing operations in the United States, these are found in North Carolina, Alabama, Mississippi, and Washington. Hawaii also has small 1- to 10-acre (0.4- to 4-hectare) tea plantations, but their success models rely as much on tourism and sheer novelty as on high volume output.

Tea plants can be grown as ornamental garden plants and houseplants, with seeds widely available from online sources, in virtually any location.

HOW TEA IS GROWN & HARVESTED

In a wild or uncultivated state, tea plants can grow for hundreds of years and attain tree-size status. Practical considerations tied to harvesting, however, induce tea farmers to keep them trimmed to accessible heights. In most of its cultivated range, tea estates (also called plantations) feature neat rows of plants that are no taller than 4 to 5 feet (1.2 to 1.5 m).

In addition to a warm climate (zone 8 climates or warmer), tea plants require at least 50 inches (130 cm) of rainfall per year and prefer acidic soils in order to thrive. Many high-quality tea plants are cultivated at elevations of 6,000 feet (1,830 m) or higher; the plants grow more slowly at these heights, but they also acquire a better flavor.

Terroir is a French term used to describe the combination of soil, climate, altitude, and latitude for plants grown in a specific region. The impact of terroir is as significant for tea plants as it is with wine, coffee, and other specialty crops. A unique terroir delivers an unparalleled "sensory signature" to the teas produced in a given region, and even from a specific hilltop or plateau.

Tea in the modern age is typically grown from cuttings taken from mature plants, or clones that are mass-produced for uniformity. After an initial period of nurturing in greenhouses or nursery beds, the young plants are set in rows that are typically about 3 feet (1 m) apart. Depending on the local climate and other conditions that affect growth, individual plants are placed from 4 to 5 feet (1.2 to 1.5 m) apart. As the plants grow, they are trained into flat-topped shapes to facilitate harvest; the top of a mature tea plant is called a "plucking plateau." Lung pruning, a specialized pruning procedure, prepares a tea plant for its ultimate mission: to produce a vibrant crop of new, tender leaves destined for an optimum harvest.

Plucking the leafset.

HARVESTING TEA

In most growing zones, it takes from three to five years for a tea plant to mature from initial planting to harvest. Everything about the quality of tea leaves is related to the nature of the leaves that are selected for harvest. The newest, uppermost leaves are prized for their taste; this new growth has the highest level of nutrients and flavor-producing compounds. For the finest white teas, the single outermost bud is selected. Only the top 1 to 3 inches (2.5 to 7.5 cm) of the mature plants are picked.

Harvesting tea leaves is a labor-intensive process. As one leaf bud emerges and slowly unfurls, the branch continues to grow and prepare for the emergence of another leaf bud. Plucking consists of harvesting the newest growth of tea leaves that have emerged from the end of the branches, called the "flush." The pluck—skillfully snapping off the top leaves and sometimes a new bud—is done by workers walking among rows of tea bushes. Deciding how much to pluck with each successive pass through the tea fields is a complex process and favors experienced workers. Market demands and the condition of the tea bush are considered, among other factors, and influence how much tea is plucked with each successive harvest.

Depending on the method of harvest and the intended market, pieces of other, older leaves may be included along with the more desirable leafset. For varieties prized for their flavor, first flush harvests are usually preferred.

Traditionally, handpicking is the harvest method of choice, as only the newest leaves—at the top, outermost stems—are plucked, and the tea pickers' task is made much more effective if they don't have to bend over or reach up while they perform this task. Waist-high bushes are ideal. In the modern era, many large tea estates, primarily in Argentina and Japan, have shifted to mechanical harvesting, which adds additional emphasis to the height of the tea bushes.

MACHINE PLUCKING

Machine plucking is generally a more cost-efficient option for some producers, but it does not yield the same quality of raw leaf material as hand-plucked teas. Machine plucking includes more stems; lower, older leaves; and is a generally inconsistent pluck. Japan's process is a notable exception. Almost all teas in Japan are harvested by machines, precisely calibrated, and utilized without adversely affecting the quality. Argentina almost exclusively harvests its commodity-grade black teas using hand-operated machines.

An industrious human plucker can gather as much as 75 pounds (34 kg) of fresh tea leaves a day. Generally, it takes about 2,000 leafsets from a Chinese variety tea plant to equal one pound of fresh leaves.

MATCHA

One of the most specialized of all teas is matcha, a traditional specialty tea produced only in Japan. Matcha is a finely powdered green tea produced from only a few varieties of tea plants. These plants have been carefully bred for hundreds of years just for this end use. Teas destined for matcha, unlike other traditional leaf teas, end their growing cycles in the shade. From small farms to large plantations, these teas are covered by netting for the last few weeks before harvest. The nets allow some light to filter in, but produce enough shade that the growing cycle in the plant changes, especially in the newly emerging leaves.

Leafsets from Assam varieties are larger and heavier; 2,000 freshly harvested leafsets of these varieties weigh about 2 pounds (0.9 kg).

There are records of wild tea plants with life spans of hundreds of years, but in agricultural use, most are considered to produce effectively for 40 to 100 years (the former is typical of Assam-type varieties, common in India; the latter is standard for Chinese varieties).

Harvest in many growing zones is an ongoing operation, spanning weeks, months, and more. The fastest-growing tea plants—the pace of growth relates to climate and altitude, amongst other factors—can produce harvestable new leaves every one to two weeks. At the highest altitudes, slower growth produces a growing season that is much shorter and, typically, only occurs in the spring. Commercial production of tea has always been linked to growing conditions, though agricultural science—both ancient and modern—has allowed profitable production in a much larger area than its original home turf in Asia; most of the choicest teas are grown at higher altitudes.

TEA PRODUCTION

Tea production is also heavily linked to the availability and cost of labor, even in the early periods of its commercial development. On average, an acre of land requires the labor of one-and-a-half to two skilled workers, for planting, crop management, and plucking. Over the last 100 years, higher yielding plants and improved crop management have

THE USE OF SHADE

The major change that shading induces in tea plants destined for matcha production is an increase in the production of chlorophyll, caffeine, tannins, vitamin C, and some amino acids, especially L-theanine. The dried and powdered leaves yield a brightly colored beverage—the green tint can be almost fluorescent—with a sweeter, more distinctive green tea flavor than conventional teas.

raised production of Assam variety tea from an average of 400 to 1,000 pounds per acre (180 to 454 kg per 0.4 hectare). At the more extreme end, some tea plantations have recorded harvests of 1,500 pounds or more per acre (680 kg per 0.4 hectare).

One of the primary characteristics that make tea a tasty, sought-after beverage is flavor. This flavor—as well as the nutritional components of tea—is directly associated with the young growth concentrated in newly emerged leaves. The compounds produced by tea to support growth include classes of chemicals that are natural growth stimulants and others that are natural insect repellents. However, despite the presence of the latter, pest control is an ongoing part of tea agriculture. The number of species of insects that attack tea is estimated to be at least 150, with most of the threat in Asia and the least in Africa.

Other threats to growing tea plants include fungi and diseases related to damp conditions. Worldwide, an estimated 380 types of disease related to fungus have been identified. Together, insects and disease destroy almost 70 million pounds (32 million kg) of tea every year. In response, tea growers, like farmers elsewhere, rely on pesticides, fungicides, and other chemical weapons to reduce their losses.

With growing concern about environmental damage and toxicity in food and beverage products, consumers may become increasingly wary of the origin and quality of teas. Tea growers and packagers in recent decades have responded with organic sourcing, testing, and labeling to ensure this kind of quality. In northern Japan, the 2011 tsunami and subsequent nuclear reactor disaster and resulting radiation leaks has also had an effect, triggering widespread testing and enhanced quality control, even though little or no contamination of Japanese teas has been documented.

After harvest, the plucked leaves are transported to a local processing factory to be weighed and sorted. The leaves are commonly cleaned by hand to remove unwanted debris, such as twigs and stones, before entering the next phases of processing.

TEA PROCESSING

The process of producing tea requires many important steps, each one involving physical and biochemical transformations, taking tea from raw, green leaf material to finished tea leaf product. These steps include withering, rolling and breaking, oxidization, firing (drying), and sorting (grading). The type of tea being made—black, oolong, green, or white—determines the specific stages of processing applied to the leaves and even the order in which they are applied. Thus, the number of processing steps and the order of these steps varies for different teas.

WITHERING

Most types of tea (black, oolong, green, and white) go through an initial stage called "withering," a gentle process that removes moisture. After the leaves are plucked from the tea plant, they are spread out onto large trays or screens. Withering is often conducted in open-air or closed processing areas utilizing natural breezes or gentle fans to assist the process. During the process, which can last from a couple of hours to the better part of a day, the tea leaves lose 50 to 80 percent or more of their moisture and become limp and soft, making them suitable for rolling.

During withering, tea leaves undergo innumerable biochemical changes: carbohydrates, fats, and proteins break down into simpler sugars, amino acids, and complex volatile oils (lipids), which eventually become components that contribute to flavor and aroma. As water and carbon dioxide are emitted and evaporate, the chlorophyll content decreases, and the caffeine and amino acid content increases.

The two types of tea that receive the most withering are oolong and black teas, a process that takes from 12 to 20 hours. A longer withering time plays a key role in expressing a wide diversity of chemicals, which are precursors to compounds that make up the more pronounced aromas of oolong and black teas.

TEA-PROCESSING STEPS

White Tea	Oolong Tea	Green Tea	Black Tea
Steaming (some styles)	Withering (drying)	Withering (most styles)	Withering
Withering (drying)	Rolling, shaking (bruising leaf edges)	Steaming (pan firing or oven firing)	Rolling (orthodox styles)
Rolling (some styles)	Oxidation (partial)	Rolling, drying	Oxidation (full)
Packing	Firing (pan firing or oven firing)	Packing	Firing
	Packing		Packing

ROLLING & SHAPING

In the rolling and shaping process, the leaf is rolled, crushed, or twisted, either by hand or by machine. This procedure ruptures the cell walls of the leaves, releasing enzymatic juices. The traditional hand-rolling process involves rolling the tea leaves between the hands so that the leaves become twisted, broken, and coated with the juices released from the leaves.

In mechanized rolling, tea goes through a roll-breaking machine, which separates large clumps of matted tea leaves into smaller, more consistent pieces. For black tea, the bruised leaves release some of the enzymes that initiate the oxidation process.

The most common method for producing high-volume, lower- or moderate-grade teas is called "CTC" (crush, tear, curl). Teas made from leaves that are not cut or torn are called "orthodox teas," and these are considered to be higher quality than CTC teas.

OXIDATION

Oxidation, sometimes incorrectly referred to as fermentation, is the procedure that makes black tea different from all other types of tea (green, oolong, white, and so on). The tea leaves are spread evenly in a layer that is 2 to 4 inches (5 to 10 cm) thick, on large troughs or racks with wire-mesh screen bottoms. This allows the leaves to have sufficient airflow on both top and bottom. The leaves are then left to oxidize, a process that has its own proprietary length of time for each tea operation. During this time, the leaves will lose most of their remaining moisture.

Oxidation takes places in large spaces with temperatures between 70 and 90°F (21 to 32°C) and a relative humidity of 75 to 90 percent. Oxidation times range between thirty minutes and three or more hours, depending on the ambient room temperature and the style of tea being manufactured. White and green teas are not oxidized; oolong tea is partially oxidized; black tea is fully oxidized.

FIRING

During the firing stage of processing, heat is applied to the leaf to stop the oxidation process. Firing is done by blowing hot air over the leaf or running the leaf through heat tunnels. Temperatures for firing range from 140 to 170°F (60 to 77°C) and this phase lasts from ten minutes to a maximum of one hour. The heating or firing process eradicates enzyme proteins in the tea leaves, essentially killing the enzymes so that the leaf is stable and does not mold or break down.

There are four reasons for applying heat during processing: to de-enzyme the leaves, to stop oxidation, to develop flavors during rolling and shaping, and to reduce moisture.

SORTING

Once the tea is fired, the leaves are sorted into grades of different sizes. Sorting can be done by hand or with the use of sifting screens of various mesh sizes designed to produce uniform-size pieces of the finished leaves. Quality tea leaves are commonly sorted by hand or with a combination of simple screens and manual manipulation. Leaves are usually cleaned, sorted, and sifted at the end of each production day, to create different lots with consistent leaf sizes, colors, and shapes.

SHIPPING

Tea was shipped in wooden chests after harvesting and processing well into the end of the last century. The chests displayed the country of origin, the name of the tea estate where the tea was produced, and the net weight of the contents. Tea containers of modern times use packaging that is more effective in keeping the tea fresh and protected from heat, moisture, and light. The contents are transported inside multilayered corrugated paper, and foil containers with inner plastic liners. The more high-end teas are often shipped in nitrogen-flushed bags; this helps remove oxygen. Some of the fancier teas shipped this way also have desiccant packs dropped into the bags before sealing to remove ambient moisture.

TEA-GROWING REGIONS

Tea is now a commodity grown around the world. The spread of tea crops throughout Asia and to other continents has mostly happened in the past 200 years, and is now an established part of agricultural communities in more than forty countries and every continent except Antarctica. However, while many countries grow tea, the production of commercial quantities and quality varies considerably, with output influenced by rainfall, temperature, and soil type, and favored teas influenced by tradition.

The world's largest importer and re-exporter of tea is Germany. This country grows no tea of its own, but has a well-developed network of packagers adding value to the bulk tea they import from tea-producing regions. England might also be thought of as a prime world source of tea, but though tea is grown in Great Britain (in greenhouses and in small quantities), the country is best known for its packaged tea products, long established within this tea-passionate culture.

AFRICA

Tea plants were introduced in Africa in the late 1800s, starting in Malawi. African regions with equatorial climates are a prime territory for tea, and Africa is now a major exporter, generating more than 30 percent of worldwide tea exports. The African teas are generally richer, darker brews with plenty of full body and strong flavor, but not a lot of complexity. This makes them popular in hearty breakfast and afternoon tea blends. Kenya leads the way producing large quantities of teas that are used in mass-market tea bags, and it is one of the world's top five "super producer" tea nations. Much of the Kenyan tea crop is grown in the highlands on both sides of the Great Rift Valley at high altitudes ranging from 5,000 to 9,000 feet (1,525 to 2,745 m). Kenyan tea is valued in the world marketplace for its consistency, competitive price, and value.

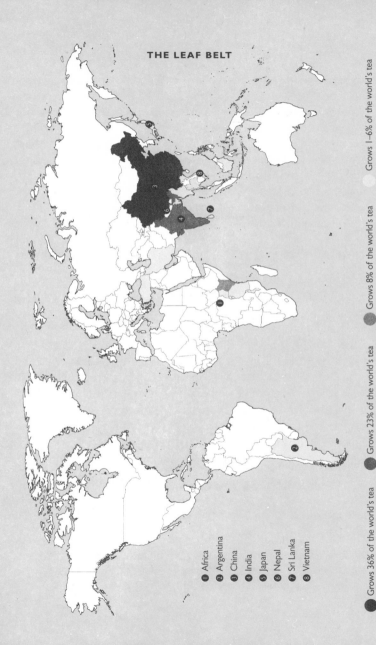

THE LEAF BELT

① Africa
② Argentina
③ China
④ India
⑤ Japan
⑥ Nepal
⑦ Sri Lanka
⑧ Vietnam

● Grows 36% of the world's tea

● Grows 23% of the world's tea

● Grows 8% of the world's tea

○ Grows 1–6% of the world's tea

ARGENTINA

Argentina entered the "tea age" in the 1960s, adding large tea-growing operations to its well-established production of wine, olive oil, and yerba maté. Black tea is the principal output of Argentina's tea farms, which are concentrated in the hot, humid highlands of the northeast. The country has been active in introducing modern, mechanized harvesting equipment, thereby expanding production and lowering costs. Argentinean black tea has a dark liquor, earthy flavor, and medium body. This tea is mostly destined for export and it is widely used in mass-market tea bags, and packaged iced-tea products used in the restaurant trade.

CHINA

It is only fitting that the motherland of tea should be the world's number-one producer of tea. China produces thousands of tea types from more than 200 dedicated tea-producing micro-regions. Tea production is largely concentrated in the southeastern provinces: Fujian, Zhejiang, Yunnan, Szechuan, Hunan, Anhui, and Hubei. The nation has more than 2.3 million acres (930,776 hectares) under cultivation spread over twenty provinces. Tea is commonly grown in small villages and taken to local co-ops for processing. China produces green, black, white, oolong, pu-erh, and various scented teas such as Jasmine and Lapsang Souchong. Green tea production accounts for approximately two-thirds of all Chinese tea production.

While China does produce more moderate-quality commercial grades of green and black tea, mostly destined for mass-market tea bags, much of the country still grows and processes finer quality specialty teas, including the desirable longer-leaf, compressed cakes styles.

The best tea-producing land in China is exceptionally diverse, with small farms and plantations ranging in altitude between 1,500 and 4,000 feet (460 and 1,220 m) at the low end, and in parts of Yunnan rising to over 6,000 feet (1,830 m).

There is no standardized protocol for naming Chinese teas, which creates a dazzling, exotic, colorful, and—at times—confusing set of choices for consumers. Many of the teas are named after local mountains and sacred agricultural enclaves, rivers, and mythical figures.

INDIA

India is a major super-producer nation for black teas, with more than 13,000 plantations (called "gardens" or "estates'") and employing more than 2 million people.

Indian black teas are known for the diversity of taste qualities including brisk, bold, and complex flavors that can be enjoyed on their own, or as part of morning or afternoon blends. While much of Indian tea is processed for mainstream teas—quantity is the goal—orthodox, traditional production is still popular. The latter targets longer leaf teas because of their higher commercial value and overall superior taste. While India exports most of its annual black tea production, Indian consumers love their black tea, brewed strong and sipped on its own with nothing added, or sometimes flavored with some ginger and other spices, sugar, and milk. Trendy American consumers will recognize this concoction as chai—rhymes with "eye." The beloved native drink of India is quickly going global.

Assam, in the northeast of the country, is the largest contiguous black tea–producing region in the world. More than 2,000 tea gardens produce a huge amount of tea annually. The moderate grades of Assam are used to make breakfast blends, packet, or bagged teas, while specialty tea connoisseurs worldwide value the finer grades of Assam.

The legendary gardens of Darjeeling are located 120 miles (193 km) to the west and north of Assam, at the foot of the majestic Himalayas. An estimated eighty-seven tea estates comprise the Darjeeling tea industry, most at elevations averaging 5,000 feet (1,525 m) above sea level. Darjeeling teas have been prized as the "champagne of teas" for decades; they offer a complex mixture of briskness—the famous "muscatel snap"—and floral astringency not found in any other teas. Both Assam and Darjeeling are home to certified organic tea estates. Labor unrest and weather calamities have nagged at these regions since their inception, yet they somehow manage to continue producing teas that command respect among tea lovers globally. Most of the Darjeeling teas are purchased by Europeans—primarily Germans—who are also big fans of organic Darjeeling teas. Germany constitutes the single largest market for Darjeeling tea.

JAPAN

Green tea is by far the most significant type of tea grown and processed in Japan, in both quality and quantity. The nation's population embraces green tea as its favorite beverage, straight or in a colorful mix of variations, blends, and ready-to-drink (RTD) selections. Japan is one of the world's top RTD tea consumer countries; increasingly the Japanese also drink black and oolong teas.

Japan is famous for its fine, needle-style leaf teas. At least 80 percent of all Japanese tea production is sencha, gyokuro, and hojicha, prime examples of this variety. Some scientific research suggests that the high consumption of green tea by the Japanese may be partially responsible for their longevity; Japan's population has the world's longest life expectancy.

An estimated 600,000 "farming families" produce most of Japan's green tea. Automated harvesting has been perfected in Japan, but some gathering of the tea leaves is still done by hand, favored traditionally as the right way to select only the appropriate leaves for harvest. Harvested tea is processed in semi- and fully-automated factories using impeccable quality-control standards.

The characteristics of Japanese tea are its vegetal, mildly grassy, and yet rarely bitter flavors. The color range is striking, ranging from dull or jade to bright, almost phosphorescent green.

NEPAL

Nepal is a small tea-growing center, focused mostly on black tea. Primarily the local population enjoys the country's annual production and little is exported. A lack of business infrastructure and decades of political strife have made tea farming difficult in this hilly landscape.

Some of the annual tea production is reputedly used to dilute Darjeeling tea. Darjeeling producers acknowledge that there has been more of its tea sold in world markets than was produced. Nepalese tea is quite similar in character to Darjeeling teas—understandably so, as they are geographic neighbors. Yet, in spite of the obstacles, determined Nepalese tea farmers have promoted their teas, which have begun to be sold in North American specialty tea shops and online.

SRI LANKA

Sri Lanka (formerly Ceylon) has a tea industry that took root in 1867 on a mere 19 acres (7.7 hectares) of land. Commercial production evolved from a single tea plant brought into the country from China in 1824. The first Ceylon teas were sold at a legendary London auction in 1873 and volumes rose rapidly soon after.

Sri Lanka produces black tea almost exclusively. The plant stock and agricultural technology used to establish the Sri Lankan tea industry were brought in from India; the teas produced by the two nations are similar in some ways, but with unique flavor distinctions as well.

Until 1971, British companies owned 80 percent of Sri Lankan tea estates. At that time, the island's government took control of a majority of these tea ventures, leaving roughly one-third to private ownership. Tea-growing fields are at elevations between 3,000 and 8,000 feet (915 and 2,440 m), with the finest-quality teas usually grown above 4,500 feet (1,370 m). Here, in the renowned Sri Lankan highlands (with a climate similar to the Darjeeling region in India) there are six main tea-producing regions and some thirty-eight sub districts with

650 tea estates. All estates produce black tea almost exclusively. A small amount of white and green tea—less than I percent of the nation's annual output—is also produced on some estates. The flavors are brisk and bold and some have a slightly sweetish taste; the color of the brewed tea is a magnificent reddish-brown.

Sri Lankan teas are produced using both the orthodox and CTC processing methods, with the former being destined for the specialty tea trade and the latter used in blends that are more common. Orthodox black tea production is the true pride of Sri Lanka and many of their excellent teas are exceptional "self drinkers," as connoisseurs refer to them. These are teas that one brews and enjoys without the addition of milk, cream, sugar, or lemon. Many Sri Lankan CTC black teas are also the base of some fruit- and spice-flavored teas.

TAIWAN

Tea cultivation started on the island of Taiwan in 1796 (when it was called Formosa). Tea plants from China were planted on small farms at or below an altitude of 1,000 feet (305 m). Today, most Taiwanese production is dedicated to producing oolong tea (partially oxidized tea leaves), which has for many years been sold to mainland China. Recently, this flow has slowed as Taiwan refocuses its tea industry, promoting it internally so that now more than 75 percent of the Taiwanese production is consumed domestically, with the rest going to the United States and Japan.

Taiwan oolongs are among the finest specialty teas available anywhere. These oolongs exhibit the most complex sensory characteristics of all teas, providing a wide range of floral, toasty, green-vegetal, and many other delightful flavors. The higher, mountain elevation oolongs may sell for $200 or more per pound (0.45 grams), with a select set of connoisseurs eager to acquire these limited production teas.

The country produces a little more than 25,557 tons (25,000 metric tons) of its prized teas each year. Taiwan has roughly 40,000 acres (16,000 hectares) under tea cultivation, and an established support system of highly skilled tea growers and processers. Sadly, these tea craftspeople are aging and few members of the younger generations seem interested in acquiring the knowledge that has been passed down for many generations.

VIETNAM

Since the end of the Vietnam War in 1975, the country has established a foothold in the international tea market. Over the last twenty years, Vietnam has expanded from producing tea that supplied only its own people and a few regional markets, to surpassing Argentina in black tea (CTC) production by a margin of more than 20 percent. Vietnamese black teas, like their Argentinean counterparts, are average-grade black teas destined for use in mass-market blends. The overall character— the color, body, flavor, and aroma—of Argentinean and Vietnamese black teas is similar (Vietnam also produces some green tea).

TEA TOURISM

Tea lovers are increasingly adding tea-growing regions as a target for their excursions. In Japan, India, Sri Lanka, and China in particular, one can visit tea-themed festivals, as well as plantations, processing plants, museums, and tea shops. In the noted tea-growing regions of Darjeeling in Northeast India and within the highlands of Sri Lanka, resort-level accommodations are part of this trend; some estates in India are still owned by families with roots dating to the era of the British Raj.

Old-fashioned tea shops in London and rural parts of England also provide a tempting option for tourists. Other worthy geographical destinations include Nepal, Amsterdam (the Netherlands), Australia, and most recently, Hawaii.

SECTION TWO

Tea Chemistry

TEA'S CORE CONSTITUENTS

The tea leaf—fresh and dried—contains a wide array of naturally occurring chemicals: caffeine, antioxidants, amino acids, vitamins, and minerals. Through the processes of drying and carefully oxidizing—or not, in the case of white and green teas— the tea leaf transmutes these substances into not only an endless variety of flavors, colors, and aromas, but also a long list of healthy constituents. While not everything found in the dry leaf is extracted in a simple brewed infusion, many of the beneficial substances do infuse into each brew and on into the human body.

According to the Tea Association of the USA[1], there have been more than 5,600 scientific studies of tea investigating the connections between tea consumption and health. The role tea plays in supporting human health worldwide has yet to be fully understood. However, it is clear this humble drink is quite possibly the closest thing to a beverage panacea. The key constituents and nutrients in tea that may serve your well-being include antioxidants, caffeine, amino acids, vitamins, and minerals. These elements are discussed briefly below.

ANTIOXIDANTS

Antioxidants are naturally occurring substances that help prevent or delay damage caused by reactive oxygen, as well as the negative effects of reactive nitrogen species that cause harm at the cellular level. Oxidative damage at the cellular level may contribute to diseases, including cancer, heart disease, and premature aging. All teas contain various types and quantities of beneficial phenolic antioxidants.

Flavonoids are a large family of polyphenolic compounds synthesized by many plant species. They are found among foods and beverages such as tea, wine, cocoa, fruit, and vegetables. Tea is the major contributor of flavonoids in the American diet, as well as for much of

[1] As reported at the Fifth International Scientific Symposium. See www.teausa.com.

CATECHIN
$C_{15}H_{14}O_6$

the rest of the world. Flavonols are a subclass of flavonoids and account for more than 90 percent of the total flavonoid content in tea. Flavonols include catechins, theaflavins, and thearubigins. Epigallocatechin gallate (EGCG) is the primary catechin found in green tea, and theaflavins and thearubigins are the primary antioxidant agents in black tea.

White tea contains mainly simple phenolic compounds, while the post-harvest processing and firing used to produce black teas and darker oolong teas produce the more complex catechins and, ultimately, the tannin-like theaflavins and thearubigins. These compounds are also antioxidants that are being researched for their health-bestowing properties. The diversity of tea-processing methods creates an almost endless variety of such components, ranging from simple phenolics in white tea to the red tannin molecules in black tea.

Extensive science-based research suggests all tea types may possibly help reduce the risk of cancer by reducing free-radical and DNA damage, inhibiting uncontrolled cancer cell growth by promoting programmed cell death (apoptosis), and by boosting the immune system to help fend off the development of cancer cells. (The results of this research have been published in thousands of journals.)

CAFFEINE
$C_8H_{10}N_4O_2$

CAFFEINE

Caffeine is a central nervous system stimulant. It promotes mental alertness and increased reaction times and plays a role in diverse physiological, psychomotor, and cognitive performance. Caffeine is a natural component of tea and is generally considered safe when consumed in moderation. Tea, with a moderate caffeine content, is believed to help improve focus, eliminate fatigue, and sharpen mental acuity. Caffeine levels in tea vary depending upon specific origins, blends, and strength of the brew.

The polyphenol antioxidants in tea bind with caffeine when tea is infused in hot water, attenuating and slowing the release of this stimulant. The idea that tea contains as much caffeine as coffee is erroneous. A cup of tea contains about one-third of the caffeine in an average cup of filtered coffee and proportionately much less compared to an espresso. Besides a lower caffeine content than coffee (on an equivalent per serving basis) this modulating action is another reason tea produces less of a short-term energy spike than coffee, yet another desirable attribute lauded by tea lovers around the world.

L-THEANINE
$C_7H_{14}N_2O_3$

AMINO ACIDS

Tea contains an estimated twenty amino acids, with theanine being the principal one. Theanine (L-theanine) is an amino acid found almost exclusively in tea, though small amounts occur in certain mushrooms. It has been shown to have interesting psychoactive properties, as it can bind to receptors in the brain involved in neurotransmission, and it is known to increase alpha brain-wave activity. Limited, but valid, clinical research has shown L-theanine to play a role in improving cognitive performance and mental focus, as well as aiding in stress reduction. It is especially abundant in Japanese matcha, a nutrient-dense form of green tea.

VITAMINS

Tea leaves in their dried state contain vitamins A, B, C, K, and others. Of these, only the B-complex vitamins and vitamin C are soluble in water. The amount of B-complex vitamins and vitamin C that make it into each brewed cup of tea is rather small, but nonetheless helps contribute to a balanced daily diet.

MINERALS

Brewed tea contains a diversity of minerals including calcium, fluorine, magnesium, manganese, potassium, and zinc. While these are all supportive of human health, only potassium is present in appreciable quantities. Manganese is essential for body development and bone growth. Potassium is vital for maintaining body fluid levels and providing muscle support.

An old myth regarding tea consumption is that certain constituents found in tea, such as caffeine and fluoride, may weaken bones. Recent research suggests drinking tea may actually have the opposite effect. Studies conducted on older women have found that those who drank four or more cups of tea a day had improved bone density compared to women who were non–tea drinkers. Furthermore, when milk is added to tea, as enjoyed by many people in Great Britain, it becomes a rich source of calcium, also important for maintaining bone health.

A HEALTHY BEVERAGE

According to the U.S. Department of Agriculture, one cup (8 fluid ounces/240 ml) of brewed black or green tea contains no sugar, fat, fiber, or protein. Both teas contain very small quantities of the B-complex vitamins and also some potassium, manganese, and other minerals. Unsweetened brewed green and black tea are "zero calorie" beverages. Tea does help with hydrating the body. While both black and green teas contain antioxidants, there has been more research into the potential health properties of green tea. Catechins, the potent antioxidants found primarily in green tea, are known for having beneficial anti-inflammatory and anti-cancer properties. According to the Tea Association of the USA, human population studies have found that people who regularly consume three or more cups of black tea per day have a reduced risk of heart disease and stroke. These beneficial properties in black tea are likely due to the presence of antioxidant theaflavins and thearubigins.

A BIOCHEMICAL JOURNEY

The making of tea is a simple act. Add hot water to tea leaves, let them steep, strain, and serve. Yet, upon ingestion of this uniquely simple brew, a vastly complex set of biochemical reactions is set off within the brain and body. The mere act of hot water connecting with the tea leaves releases hundreds of compounds, including volatile oils, nutrients, antioxidants, and more into a tasty aqueous solution.

Not all of these compounds are fully released into the cup, but those that survive their journey into the water are soon transported into brain and body to impart their unique benefits, some independently and some in tandem with others. The color of the infusing water changes due to the impact of polyphenolic tannins and proteins. The oils trapped snugly inside the leaves are released and seep into the warm water—with some evaporating directly over the water—creating heady, exotic aromas, adding another dimension to the entire experience. There is simply nothing comparable to the subsequent feelings and sensations when one sips tea. Some report relaxation, some become energized, and others benefit from a feeling of being refreshed, poised, and clear-headed simultaneously. Quite a tall order for such a simple drink.

Depending upon various factors, including the intrinsic quality of the leaf, how tea is processed after harvesting, brew factors (steeping times, water quality), and how much of the resulting liquid is consumed, variations of solids (caffeine, nutrients, and volatile oils) from the dried leaves make it into the cup and on into your system as you imbibe.

AROMATHERAPY WITH TEA

While few tea connoisseurs list the aromatherapeutic attributes of freshly brewed tea on their list of wellness benefits, clinically trained aromatherapy experts have been taught to understand the differences. The hundreds of essential and volatile oil compounds that are found in every type of tea produce a staggeringly diverse variety of aromatic bouquets—sometimes called the "nose." A skilled aromatherapy technician will encourage tea drinkers to mindfully take in the aroma of freshly brewed tea for two reasons: to expand the full benefits of the tea's healthy volatile oils, which float above the cup, and to help lock into the brain the scents of each tea as a memory. The goal is to learn about tea beyond its sensory taste and color impressions. These same aroma compounds also contribute to the unique flavor characteristics and health benefits of each tea.

HYDRATION

Brewed tea is an important source of fluid. It contains approximately 99 percent water with the remaining 1 percent dissolved solids. The British Dietetic Association advises that tea can help meet daily fluid requirements. They furthermore proclaim that tea consumption does not produce a diuretic effect unless the amount of tea consumed at one sitting contains more than 300 mg of caffeine, the equivalent of six or seven cups of tea. Single servings of caffeine at doses of more than 300 mg may have a diuretic effect, according to some laboratory studies; however, this is more caffeine than casual tea drinkers would consume. Moreover, regular consumption of tea leads to caffeine tolerance, so the diuretic effect is diminished in people who regularly drink tea. One to two cups of coffee, on the other hand, can exceed this 300 mg threshold for caffeine.

DECAFFEINATED TEA

In 1906, a German merchant by the name of Ludwig Roselius successfully patented a decaffeination process for coffee. Offshoots of this technology were eventually applied to the decaffeination of tea, but it was not until 1980 that "decaf tea" was available worldwide. There are several ways in which tea can be decaffeinated, including supercritical fluid extraction, the ethyl acetate method, or the methylene chloride method.

Tea contains from 1.5 to 4.5 percent naturally occurring caffeine (by weight). According to the U.S. Food and Drug Administration, 97 percent of this amount must be removed in order for a consumer product label to state that the tea is decaffeinated. Some tea brands label their teas "98 percent caffeine free"; however, these teas may have never been decaffeinated but simply have a naturally low caffeine count. Or, they may possibly be mislabeled under current regulations. "Caffeine Free" labels only apply to herbal tea beverages.

Young tea leaves and buds contain more caffeine per weight than older leaves and stems. This is a natural condition, perhaps nature's way of protecting sensitive new tea growth from insect predators, which shy away from the bitter substance. Results of laboratory research suggest that a five-minute steep yields up to 70 percent of the available caffeine in a serving, and a second steep of the same leaves has one-third the caffeine of the first. Many "tea experts" state that rinsing the leaves before steeping will decaffeinate the tea, but this is a mildly controversial concept—it has little effect on caffeine content and also reduces the flavor of the resulting cup. Another common technique among tea drinkers is to discard a first, short steep—15 to 60 seconds—which will reduce some of the caffeine that remains in a subsequent, longer steep intended for drinking. However, this is at the cost of some loss of flavor. According to tea industry rumors, commercial decaffeination of tea using only water as a solvent is a potential fix.

Accurate labeling of regular teas specific to their actual caffeine content, let alone after decaffeination, is somewhat problematic; caffeine levels in conventional teas normally fluctuate from product to product, season to season, and even plant to plant. Consumers are often left to interpret how much caffeine is left in their decaffeinated tea using the percentages listed on tea labels put forth by Lipton, Celestial Seasonings, and a handful of other tea brands. The labeling effort may be sincere, but the results are not likely to be correct, or even consistent.

SUPERCRITICAL FLUID EXTRACTION

The process of decaffeinating tea using CO_2 (carbon dioxide) is sometimes called the CO_2 method, or the liquid carbon dioxide method, or the supercritical carbon dioxide method, but it is technically known as supercritical fluid extraction. In this process, tea leaves are gently doused with carbon dioxide (an inert gas) in a sealed, high-pressure (1,000 pounds per inch/454 kg per 25 mm) chamber. The supercritical CO_2 acts selectively on the caffeine, releasing the caffeine alkaloids, which bind to the gas. The gas is flushed out of the pressure chamber and the caffeine is removed through filtering. The cleansed CO_2 is reused. This process has the advantage of avoiding the use of potentially harmful substances. It is the primary method used to decaffeinate large quantities of commercial-grade, less-exotic coffee found in grocery stores.

Supercritical decaffeination is mandated as the only allowable process used on certified organic teas in the United States and Europe. This technology is expensive, but it leaves no solvent residues of any type, and reportedly preserves more of the important polyphenol antioxidants intact. This method, along with the ethyl acetate method, are the only processes allowed for decaffeinated teas imported into the United States.

SUPERCRITICAL FLUID (CO$_2$)
EXTRACTION OF CAFFEINE FROM TEA

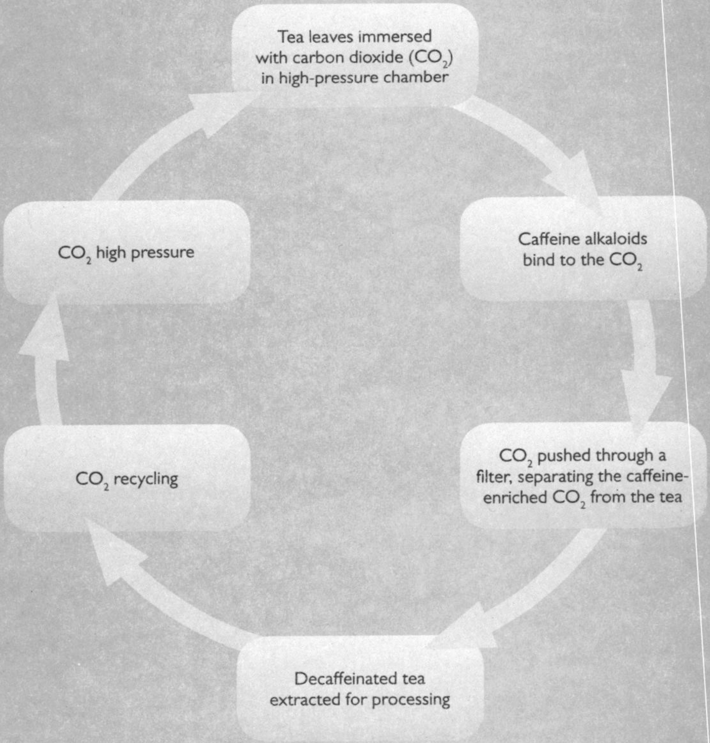

Tea leaves immersed with carbon dioxide (CO_2) in high-pressure chamber

Caffeine alkaloids bind to the CO_2

CO_2 pushed through a filter, separating the caffeine-enriched CO_2 from the tea

Decaffeinated tea extracted for processing

CO_2 recycling

CO_2 high pressure

ETHYL ACETATE METHOD

Use of ethyl acetate (EA) as a solvent to decaffeinate tea is generally considered a natural method due to its low toxicity and agreeable odor and the fact that it occurs in various fruits, vegetables, and other botanicals. Tea leaves are bathed in a process utilizing water and ethyl acetate, resulting in most, but not all, of the caffeine being removed. The solution containing the tea is then dried and packaged.

Use of EA to decaffeinate tea removes more polyphenols than super-critical fluid (CO_2) technology, and some sensitive tea tasters say they can taste a slight difference, or aftertaste, with EA-decaffeinated teas. Coffee beans are also sometimes decaffeinated with this solvent.

METHYLENE CHLORIDE METHOD

This method uses a liquid solution containing methylene chloride. The tea is bathed in the solution and the caffeine molecules in the tea are attracted to and bind with the methylene chloride molecules. The liquid is then drained off and the tea dried for packaging.

In the United States, methylene chloride is not used for decaffeinating tea, although it is allowed for coffee. Concerns by the U.S. Food and Drug Administration about residual levels of methylene chloride remaining on tea leaves after processing, and the potential harm from regular consumption of this chemical, have put it on the banned list.

However, in the European Union (EU) this method is allowed to decaffeinate tea, even though purity standards for pesticides and other contaminants in tea are much stricter there.

TEA & HEALTH

Tea has long been consumed as a refreshing beverage, but in its ancient homelands in China and India, it was first revered as a health-promoting tonic. In modern times, health and wellness have returned as functional attributes associated with tea. Increasingly, tea is regarded as healthy because it has no calories, a considerable plus in an age of copious consumption of calorie-laden drinks such as carbonated sodas.

Major health probes associated with ongoing research into the positive effects of tea include applications in cancer treatment, cardiovascular disease, diabetes, neurodegenerative diseases linked with aging (Alzheimer's and Parkinson's disease among them), and obesity. Other health-related research is aimed at promoting health—preventive— rather than fighting active disease states, including studies looking into how tea consumption may boost athletic performance and prevent diseases such as diabetes and skin cancer. In at least one study, the application of L-theanine and epigallocatechin gallate (EGCG)—natural components of tea leaves—resulted in a reduction of more than 30 percent in symptoms of the common cold and the flu.[2]

Applications of tea—both black and green teas—in cancer research include promising findings as a treatment for breast cancer, colon cancer, rectal cancer, pancreatic cancer, and some forms of skin cancer. In various studies, either tea itself or its major components— polyphenols such at EGCG—were measured for effectiveness. Though no evidence points to tea as a cure-all, the outcome of multiple science-based trials suggests that tea has diverse therapeutic effects, reducing the odds of developing certain cancers and in some cases supporting mainstream treatment protocols.

[2] *Journal of the American College of Nutrition 2007*; 26(5). 'Specific formulation of *Camellia sinensis* prevents cold and flu symptoms' pp. 445–52.

CHOLESTEROL & OBESITY

Cholesterol, a prime subject of nutritionists concerned about the ill effects of heavy fat consumption on health and longevity, has been studied as a target for tea. In one research program conducted by the U.S. Department of Agriculture, the conclusion was that "inclusion of tea in a diet moderately low in fat reduces total and LDL cholesterol by significant amounts and may, therefore, reduce the risk of coronary heart disease." A prime focus in tea-based cholesterol research studies is, as for cancer research, the potent tea component EGCG. Green tea, naturally high in this compound, is linked through consumption studies in various countries with a reduced risk from some of the negative outcomes of cholesterol consumption, and EGCG in direct application reinforces the concept that it is a potent and beneficial component of tea.

Along with cholesterol, the global issue of obesity is attracting increasing scientific interest as yet another potential way in which tea consumption may be healthy. In studies on rats, Japanese researchers concluded that the catechins extracted from green tea were effective in decreasing fat as well as lowering cholesterol. Other recent medical studies in Japan expanded this research to human subjects, and concluded that "decreases in body weight, body mass index, body fat ratio, body fat mass, waist circumference, hip circumference, visceral fat area, and subcutaneous fat area were found to be greater in the catechin group than in the control group." A few cups of tea each day combined with exercise and a balanced diet may help balance the scales—literally.

Obesity has been linked to diabetes, with increasing frequency an issue worldwide, especially in middle-class populations[3]. Once again, the catechin antioxidants in green tea provide fascinating promise. In many countries including China, Japan, the Netherlands, South Korea, Switzerland, Greece, and Taiwan, clinical research points to a positive effect from these compounds, reducing obesity related to diet and

[3] *Nature*, 2009, "Connecting obesity, aging and diabetes," pp. 996–7.

therefore lowering the risk of developing diabetes. Research studies of this type sometimes use dietary supplements made from tea extracts; others make correlative connections that compare tea drinkers within the general population. One such meta-study in China concluded "tea consumption of four or more cups a day may lower the risk of type 2 diabetes." Although catechins in green tea appear to be the primary beneficial constituent in much of this research, other nutrients and naturally occurring chemical constituents found in tea may also be of benefit, and, as some studies have concluded, exercise and active lifestyles also play a critical role.

CARDIOVASCULAR DISEASE

Numerous science-based studies conducted on tea have shown its promise as a preventive or modifying agent in cardiovascular diseases, including strokes and heart attacks. In both Japan and the United States, researchers have shown that the consumption of green tea is associated with lowering the risk of heart attacks and reducing mortality from both heart attacks and stroke. In some of these studies, black tea as well as green tea has been shown to be effective. (See the bibliography for further information.)

AGE & HEALTH

In the United States, as in many other areas of the world, an aging population is frequently correlated with increased health problems. Among these are rising rates of cognitive impairments directly linked with aging, chief among them Alzheimer's disease. Researchers in various tea-centric research projects have explored the value of green tea and a few of its major components—particularly EGCG and theanine—on specific types of age-related health issues. Consumption of green tea in general suggests that depression and depressive symptoms in the elderly are reduced (Japan); and the risk of developing

Parkinson's disease may also be reduced (Finland, India, Israel). Some of the effects of Alzheimer's and related cerebrovascular diseases may be prevented (Japan, United States).

Scientific research may provide a clue as to why this occurs. As observed earlier, tea consumption has been associated with a sense of calmness, a reduction of psychological stress, and improvement of cognitive function. While the latter is linked to the caffeine in tea, the component related to its calming attributes is L-theanine.

While L-theanine on its own has a positive record in medical studies, research has not yet fully proved evidence of its role in tea for reducing stress, improving quality of sleep, or, in some popular claims, reducing menstrual discomfort. A major study from the European Food Safety Authority reported in 2011[4] that all of these claims were unsubstantiated by existing research. On the other hand, also in 2011, a different meta-study concluded that the combination of L-theanine and caffeine (as occurs naturally in tea) resulted in positive effects on alertness, calmness, and contentedness, at least in some research projects. The combination of L-theanine and caffeine may be the key, improving brain activity and reducing some of the negative effects of overstimulation associated with caffeine. "Jittery nerves" are a commonly reported problem with coffee drinkers.

As with many health and wellness trends in modern society, hype and myth often accompany reality. There is rational support for many health benefits associated with regular tea consumption and a long history of its safe use. In the frenzy to capitalize on the health benefits reported from the scientific research community, unsubstantiated claims are also sometimes put forth recklessly by brands, bloggers, and even enthusiastic tea drinkers. Enjoy your tea, but don't expect it to be a cure-all.

[4] *EFSA Journal* 2011; 9(6): 2238.

Tea & Taste

CATEGORIES OF TEA

Regardless of origin, cultivar, or processing method, there are five primary categories of tea recognized in the Western hemisphere: green tea, black tea, white tea, oolong, and pu-erh. In addition to the five primary tea types, there are countless others that originate in various countries—for example, yellow tea from China and purple tea from Africa—but these are limited to popularity within their native regions.

The post-harvesting processing for each of these teas determines the amount of oxidation, color (as both a dry leaf and as a brewed infusion or "liquor"), and flavor. As the tea leaves oxidize, polyphenols and enzymes are transformed into complex tea polyphenols, thereby changing the antioxidant content that boosts certain nutrient levels (L-theanine is one of the most prominent) and making significant shifts in leaf color, texture, and flavor. The ultimate taste of the tea is why processing after harvest is so vital to cup quality.

BLACK TEA

Black tea originated in ancient China, though this country is predominately a green tea producer and consumer (along with white, oolong, and others). Sri Lanka, India, Africa, and South America are now the world's top black tea–producing countries. In Sri Lanka and India, the people consume black teas almost exclusively. In much of Asia, black tea is known as "red tea," based on the color of the brewed infusion—reddish-golden, darker yellow, orange, and sometimes even rather black. Precision oxidation of freshly picked tea leaves cures the leaves to these coppery-red, black, and brown colors, but many other factors may also be involved.

Black tea

Classic black teas from India are the legendary Assams, which are hearty, bold, and strong, and Darjeelings, unique among black teas with their muscatel grape–like finish, a dry, fruity snap. Sri Lanka is famous for its high-mountain black teas that are also hearty, bold, and strong, yet many have a wonderful, sublime sweetness or "top notes" (the flavors perceived first). Kenyan black teas are utilized worldwide as base teas to add strength, color, and body, while other, more complex teas are often added for their top-note attributes. South American black varieties are strong, astringent, and have little complexity; they are popular in mass-market retail and food service teas, usually in blends. China's black teas, in numerous styles and flavors, run the gamut from the ultra-rich, bold, almost syrupy Keemuns to peppery Yunnan teas and countless others.

Black teas make up all of the world's classic breakfast teas, and most of those served at high tea and afternoon tea services. Black teas generally respond nicely to a small splash of milk or cream, with the exception of Darjeeling and higher-end Chinese black teas such as Yunnan. The ever-popular spiced chai tea is made from black tea and spices, simmered or steeped together, with sugar and milk often added in North American versions of this classic Indian tea beverage.

Green tea

GREEN TEA

Green tea is mainly produced in China, Japan, Korea, and parts of Southeast Asia and harvested each year between March and late May. Green tea was largely consumed only in Asia until the last couple of decades, but it is now exceptionally popular in North America and Europe, with imports into these regions growing each year. Skilled application of steam, heat from processing ovens, sunlight, and other techniques halt the vast majority of oxidation within the freshly plucked leaves, leaving plentiful antioxidants and the fresh, clean flavor intact.

For many years, green tea was thought to contain less caffeine than black tea, but recent analytical testing indicates caffeine levels in green tea—and white tea as well—can be comparable and even exceed the amount found in comparable servings of strong black tea. Conversely, the reduced processing applied to produce green tea in comparison to black tea results in prolific levels of antioxidants. Among the better-known green teas are Chinese Dragonwell (Long Jin), Japanese sencha, and various scented jasmine teas, including the novel jasmine pearls—tightly rolled little balls of green tea delicately laced with jasmine scent.

Green tea was the commodity dumped into Boston Harbor during the infamous Boston Tea Party of 1773, but the United States, like Great Britain, has preferred black tea over green since the 1800s.

WHITE TEA

Researchers have discovered that some white teas have the highest antioxidant content of any teas. White tea consists of tea leaves that are withered and dried; no firing, heating, or rolling is applied. The leaves used for white tea are the downy, fuzzy top bud of an emerging leaf and the two emerged leaves next to it. These are harvested by hand each spring. The flavor of white tea is exceptionally mild, with a light, almost honey-like sweetness, and a dilute finish. Brewed white tea is not white, but a pale yellow color. Fans of brisk, bold black and oolong teas, or the more vegetal greens might be disappointed by comparison, but white tea is universally revered by tea connoisseurs, who praise its subtle nuances. It should be brewed strong.

China was the first to produce white teas. Two prominent varieties are the long leaf White Peony and Silver Needles; the latter is so-called because the dried leaves look like long, silver-gray needles. White teas can be produced from tea plants anywhere in the world, but it will be a long time before any country can compete with China for this elite category. White tea made its first big splash in the United States during the late 1990s.

White tea

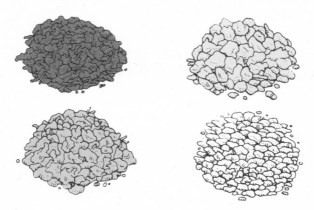

A variety of oolong teas from China and Taiwan

OOLONG TEA

Many people have heard of oolong tea, but few people can define it. Oolong teas can be either partially oxidized, a lighter processing style that makes it resemble a green tea, or heavily oxidized, giving them the taste, look, and feel of a black tea. Oolong originated in China and spread to Taiwan. Tea plants used to manufacture just about any tea can also be used to produce oolong, but the special processing used is considered a high-art form. Mastery of this skill takes many years to perfect. Oolong teas undergo more individual steps in processing than any other tea type, including withering, oxidizing, special leaf bruising, rolling, more oxidation (in some types), and repeated firing or roasting to lock in aromas and flavors.

Oolong teas have amazing complexity in flavor, aroma, and appearance. Leaf color and brewed tea liquor run the spectrum from dark-coffee brown to amber-orange, golden-yellow, and beyond. China's Eastern Beauty and Wuyi Oolong teas are two types that are revered by connoisseurs and collectors, much like fine wines. The high mountain Taiwanese oolongs such as Jade Oolong and Ali Shan are bought, sold, and collected like exotic single-malt whiskeys and rare artwork. Global demand is increasing but, with limited production, prices are rising.

PU-ERH TEA

Originating in China's Yunnan province, pu-erh dates back more than 2,000 years. This somewhat rare form of tea is the stuff of legend, lore, mystery, and even counterfeiting. Tea experts rarely concur on how exactly pu-erh is processed, but we do know Sheng pu-erh is greenish and raw leaf, whereas Shu pu-erh is made from a ripened leaf (or black tea). Both are processed by hand, compressed into round discs, and aged in darkness for months, or even decades. Some suggest this strange tea is inoculated with local microorganisms that boost ripening and health benefits; caves where it is aged may be where it absorbs health-supportive prebiotic and probiotic pathogens.

The aged pu-erh cakes sell in cycles worldwide with collectors driving prices high one year, while the next year's prices drop, much as with coffee, oil, and other commodities. The flavor is most certainly an acquired taste—it resembles no other beverages—something like an aged blue cheese with a woodsy, mossy component. You should try to purchase pu-erh from an experienced, well-known tea merchant, because fake pu-erh, which is artificially aged, is quite common in the tea world. Some health and wellness practitioners recommend pu-erh for weight management and control of high cholesterol, and there is limited, but promising science behind these potential health benefits.

Pu-erh tea

TEA BLENDING

Tea tasters may work on a single farm, with a tea importer using imported tea stock, or at the brand level. They work diligently to put their teas into distribution with very consistent flavor profiles. This consistency is only possible through skillfully created blends that match a standard—often set by the wholesaler—before they are moved on to tea merchants and brands. Not only does blending deliver the consistency consumers expect, but also blended teas are far more affordable than the single origin teas that are produced in much smaller volumes than mass-market teas of commerce; and which command a premium price. Some tea-producing regions are well-known for single origin greens, others for black and oolong varieties.

SINGLE ORIGIN TEAS

When teas from various cultivars are processed without blending, they are known as "single origin" teas. These teas are prized for numerous novel traits, including brewed tea strength, complexity of flavor, special aromas, and even nutritional attributes such as L-theanine content. The single origin teas are also processed using long-standing methods that are proprietary to the farm or estate. The combination of unique cultivars and novel processing methods makes these single origin teas highly treasured by tea buyers and consumers. Each has a special set of sensory traits found only in the single origin—and nowhere else.

BLENDED TEAS

Blended, flavored, and scented teas are commonplace in the tea marketplace. In fact, blended teas are the norm worldwide. Formulation of elegantly blended, flavored, and scented teas is a skill requiring years of experience and endless experimentation. While anyone can create their own custom blends, the experienced tea blend master, like a skilled perfumer or wine master, is able to combine disparate elements into a cohesive and highly desirable beverage.

Tea blenders create final batches of a
specific tea by tasting various different teas that
are laid out together in lines. They then recommend
the ideal proportions of each tea to be used in the
specific blend, using the covered pots to
indicate their preferences.

There are two types of blended teas. The first are mass-market blends—black or green are the most common—which tea experts create for tea bags and some loose teas. If you were not aware of them, you might think a given tea was simply made from one specific type of tea, but the fact is your daily cup might consist of a few teas from different regions and in some cases, different countries. For example, one blend may contain Kenyan and South American tea leaves as well as tea from China. These are artfully mixed to balance cup character: flavors, aromas, colors, and more.

The candidate teas are assessed individually by the tea blend master, who then mixes the teas he or she feels might best contribute to the final blend. This process might take hours, days, or weeks, until the perfect blend is realized. A large sample of the chosen "master reference blend" is kept on hand for ongoing comparison, helping to maintain consistency over time.

The second type of blend that forms part of this category is the ever-popular breakfast blend (for example, Irish, English, and Scottish). These are made from single or multiple teas used as a base with either flavorings or scents mixed in; both flavor and scent may be added in some products.

Teas with added flavorings, scents, and decorative flowers have become exceptionally popular in North America. Some tea connoisseurs scoff at the idea of adding anything to tea, much as a wine sommelier might look upon a fruited punch (sangria) or blended wine. Regardless, much of the world enjoys flavored and scented teas.

Vanilla beans and lemon balm

FLAVORED TEAS

When making blended teas, the formulator or blend master will decide upon a base tea or blend of teas that it is felt will best "carry" the addition of various flavors. The flavors or essences are either extracted from natural materials, such as spices, herbs, and fruits, or synthesized from artificial chemicals, which closely mimic natural flavors. In the United States, a flavoring must be labeled as either "natural," if it is extracted from natural materials and has nothing artificial or synthetic added, or "artificial" if it is unnatural. In the European Union (EU), flavors may be called "natural"—if they are—or "natural identical" in the case of artificial or synthetic flavorings.

The most popular flavored tea in the world is Earl Grey. This product was named after a British prime minister from the 1830s, the original Lord Earl Grey. It is a blend of strong black tea flavored with essence or extract of bergamot, a member of the citrus family.

Flavored teas often contain decorative dried flowers—calendula, hibiscus, marigold, and others—along with the flavoring component. Small pieces of dried fruits and even nuts may be added. The decorative flowers rarely add any flavor; they are blended in for aesthetic beauty. Vanilla-flavored black tea may contain very small pieces of vanilla beans along with either natural or artificial vanilla flavorings. Some flavored teas contain a primary flavor as well as an array of other flavors that support the primary flavor aromas (referred to as the "notes"), but hide in the background of the flavor array. Flavored teas are usually drunk hot, but make good iced teas as well.

SCENTED TEAS

Scented teas are often mistakenly referred to as flavored teas. While they do impart flavors and aromas that are beyond that of the tea base, technically speaking this added character comes from various aromatic botanicals, not fruits or spices. Aromatic botanicals, in contact with the tea for a short period, release volatile aromatic oils onto tea leaves, gently impregnating the leaves.

The world's most popular scented tea is jasmine, which is most often made with a green tea base (and occasionally with oolong), and then scented with either fresh or dried jasmine flower petals. Other popular scented teas include chrysanthemum, magnolia, osmanthus, and rose.

In China, where jasmine tea was invented, green tea is harvested in the spring and stored until August, when jasmine flowers are in bloom and ready to harvest. Mature jasmine flowers ooze with a heady, floral essence. The flowers are layered between and around the green tea, and held together for many hours, a complex, laborious, and expensive process. The classic Chinese jasmine green tea called Yin Hao Jasmine is produced in this manner, but cheap imitations are manufactured with artificial jasmine flavor sprayed over low-quality green tea leaves. Sometimes a few of the wilting, pretty white jasmine flowers are artfully blended into the finished mix to add a nice visual appearance; a similar process is used to make rose-scented teas and other variations.

Jasmine tea

SMOKED TEAS

Legend and lore abound regarding the invention of the first smoked teas. Some suggest it was purely accidental, arising when black teas were carried by horseback on the legendary Silk Road trails in Northern China and were exposed to smoke from nightly campfires. Others hint that in the early 1800s, Chinese tea processors tried to find ways to expedite the drying and firing of tea leaves using racks placed over open fires; the resulting "smoked teas" had no appeal to locals but caught on with Europeans and Russians who strongly fancied the smoky creations. Lapsang Souchong is the best known of these teas. For novice tea drinkers, it is most definitely an acquired taste.

Lapsang Souchong tea

BREWED TEA

Experienced tea tasters, or "cuppers," as they call themselves, consider the scent or aroma of tea to be as important as tasting for assessing the flavor of freshly brewed samples. As tea is brewed, the many oils and other compounds that make up the unique aromatic signature of each brew are released into the water. Some of these volatile oils escape into the air and, by smelling them, the taster starts to piece together the profile of that brew.

Some of these oils and complex biochemical essences evaporate rapidly during brewing, making it important to smell the tea as it brews, not just when the leaves have been removed. Other oils and essences remain in suspension and are part of the entire tasting experience; they travel across the tongue, into nasal passages, and on into the brain, where they become part of a personal aroma "memory bank" that expands as more and more tea is sampled over time. A tea taster will tell you that the aroma of brewed tea can unlock the mystery and quality of the tea nearly as much as the tasting reveals. "The nose knows" is a common expression in the world of tea aroma assessment.

THE FEEL OF THE DRY LEAF

Aroma, taste, and even the feel of brewed tea in the mouth (referred to as "mouthfeel" in the food and beverage industries) are vital sensory assessment points. Holding and touching dried tea leaves provides another indicator of quality. Dried tea leaves should be ever-so-pliable, not crumbling too easily when gently rubbed on the palms, or even somewhat soft or leathery. If the leaves crumble quite easily or emit dust and very fine particles, it is likely that the leaves were dried improperly or the tea is past its prime.

AROMA DESCRIPTORS

These are some of the many terms used by tea tasters to indicate unique characters of the aroma of a tea sample.

AROMATIC Rich in aroma, scent, and fragrance.

BOUQUET Plentiful aromas, with more than one scent coming through when inhaled.

BURNT OR BAKED Exhibiting an off note (of flavor or aroma) that is reminiscent of burnt or baked fiber. This characteristic is due to over-firing and removing too much moisture during the post-harvest processing of tea leaves.

COMPLEX Tea that is rich in desirable scents, including profound basic aromas and subtle top-notes.

FLOWERY OR FLORAL Scent as perceived in the mouth and nasal passageways that is similar to the smell of fresh-cut flowers.

FRESH The aromatic essence that gives off an overall impression of freshness, including lighter scents that are reported as "simply inspiring."

FRUITY Commonly used to describe lightly oxidized oolong teas that emit aromas often compared to various seed fruits, such as nectarines, peaches, pears, and plums.

GRASSY A grass-like smell that may indicate a pleasant green tea.

HAY-LIKE A hay-like aroma may indicate a tea that has gone "off" during processing or storage; simply not desirable.

HEADY Rich in aroma, complex, and evocative of diverse scent memories.

SMOKY In the case of wood-scented tea such as Lapsang Souchong, an almost tar-like aroma. But for other teas, hints of smoke often mean poor handling during the heating stage of processing.

SPICY A zesty aroma that is acceptable only if it is subtle; more common to oolong than black or green teas. An aroma with too much spice smell could mean improper storage of the tea, which has allowed odor contamination.

VEGETAL Brewed tea that emits the aroma of a grassy or fresh-mown lawn. If not too overpowering, indicative of some green teas.

WOODY, EARTHY Aromas reminiscent of wet wood, earth, and associated natural elements. These are expected in an aged tea such as pu-erh. In stronger black teas, however, it may indicate either very old tea or tea that has been contaminated during processing or in storage.

BREWED TEA DESCRIPTORS

These are some of the many terms used by tea tasters to indicate unique characters in the taste of a tea sample.

ASTRINGENCY The various oils and tannins in tea add a pleasant "bite" to flavor in better quality teas. A harsh astringency, even bitterness, however, may indicate low tea grades. The balance of astringency against softer aspects of a tea creates a desirable character, also referred to as "guts," "strength," "base," and sometimes, "body."

BODY Tactile sensations of weight and viscosity once tea is inside the mouth, as created by soluble solids in the brewed cup. Thin, medium, thick, or full-bodied are terms used to describe the relative levels of mouthfeel. A body that is too thin may be overly wispy, while a body that is too thick may feel overly heavy in the mouth.

BRISK The opposite of flat (see below); more than simple pungency, a brisk tea is somewhat "alive" in the mouth. Used when describing black teas. A nicely brisk black tea awakens the senses with boldness and a balanced assertiveness of flavor.

COMPLEX Some of the higher-quality teas in the world exhibit a desirable complexity of both nose (aroma) and flavor. Complex in this application represents an almost indescribable mélange of flavors working in concert.

FINISH The final part of the sensory impact in the mouth.

FLAT An absence of briskness, usually as applied to black teas. This attribute may be caused by tea that is overly aged.

FRESH Teas with a certain spring-like quality or brightness. Usually applied to teas that are recently processed or perhaps a little acidic.

FULL BODIED Stronger, full-flavor infusions, usually in black or oolong teas, which yield a pleasant strength, moderate briskness, and non-bitter character, often with a smooth finish.

HIGH GROWN Teas grown at high elevations that are often more complex and sublime than those produced at low altitudes.

MALTY Heartier black teas, usually from Assam in India or parts of Sri Lanka, which display a note of subtle sweetness combined with the attributes of a fresh grain.

MUSCAT Used exclusively when describing the flavor, and aroma, of finer Darjeeling teas. A light, fruity flavor with a classic "snap," or finish, similar to that of a ripe, muscatel-like grape.

PUNGENT A tea with a pleasant astringency, without bitterness or a rough mouthfeel.

SHORT Flavors that start nicely but fade rapidly; not a desirable trait.

SWEET In strong black or oolong teas, a sublime sweetness is a perfect counter-balance to intense boldness, briskness, and astringency.

TANNIC A balanced tea that creates a warm, pleasant flavor, and perfect astringency.

THIN Watery, wispy teas proclaiming no definitive traits of character.

WATERY Brewed tea that is little different than tasting warm water. This can be the case for old, stale teas that have lost all of their volatile oils, and other flavor components. There may be a nice color and even a light aroma, but flavor is simply absent.

THE LANGUAGE OF TEA

Learning the basic language of tea is a simple exercise, though it may feel a bit daunting at first. Unlike human languages and dialects that vary from country to country, tea terminology is not standardized. Yet tea tasters worldwide generally apply similar terminology to facilitate trade among themselves, especially when describing brewed tea, called the tea "liquor" by professional tasters around the world.

The system of using acronyms to describe tea is applicable to the loose dried leaves (sometimes called "bulk") and differs between the two main categories: black tea and green tea. For black teas, however, some of the same terms are often used within the tea trade when describing green and oolong leaf styles.

The acronym system is primarily used in India, Africa, and Sri Lanka, whereas in China and most other tea regions, localized names are preferred. The acronyms OP, BOP, BOPF only refer to the leaf size and style—also known as the "cut"—and are not necessarily a reference to quality, which is associated with flavor, color, or aroma. As one well-known tea importer once proclaimed, "The more letters, usually the higher quality and costlier tea." For example, TGFOP stands for Tippy Golden Flowery Orange Pekoe, a very high-quality tea; BOPF for Broken Orange Pekoe Fannings, a high-quality tea; and PF represents Pekoe Fannings, a tea of lesser quality.

While there are many more acronyms than these used in the tea trade, not all of these abbreviated terms are recognized by consumers; however, they are used for communication among increasingly sophisticated buyers at all levels. Understanding these key acronyms will help improve your own communication with knowledgeable tea merchants, as well as make interpretation of product labels clearer.

WHOLE DRY BLACK TEA

FLOWERY Refers to extremely fine leaf tips and buds, not the flowers of the tea plant.

GOLDEN Color of new tea leaves (the flush) as they start to emerge.

ORANGE PEKOE (OP) Long tea leaves, sometimes thin and a bit wiry, these are generally of higher quality than smaller leaves. The "Orange" in Orange Pekoe is thought to be an homage to an old Dutch tea-trading house. OP tea leaves are suitable for brewing in either teapots or infusers; they are sometimes used in better quality tea bags.

PEKOE (P) Moderate-sized tea leaves for loose brewing, sometimes used in tea bags.

SOUCHONG Broad, rounder, long leaves from lower on the plant, common to some Chinese teas.

TIPPY The ends or tips of the newest tea leaves, golden-orange in hue, and revered by connoisseurs.

BROKEN DRY TEA

BROKEN ORANGE PEKOE (BOP) Small particles of tea leaves (also called "brokens") commonly used in tea bags and included in many black tea breakfast blends. These may contain some tips and are a base for many black tea blends worldwide.

DUST (D) The smallest particles of tea leaf, used exclusively in low-grade tea bags and for production of some liquid tea concentrates.

FANNINGS (F) Smaller particles of tea leaves, about $\frac{1}{32}$ inch (1 mm) in diameter, used only in tea bags; may also be called Broken Orange Pekoe Fannings.

GREEN DRY TEA

Green teas generally have their own terminology distinct from that used with black teas, covering not only leaf sizes but also the firing style used for production. In Japan and China, green teas may be referred to as "pan-fired" (not "pan-fried," as they are often erroneously named) or "basket-fired."

Many China green teas are named after mountains, springs, sacred rivers, and the like. For example, Lung Ching ("Dragonwell"), and Pi Lo Chun ("Green Couch Spring"). The lack of even basic, intra-country standardization for green tea dry leaf terms makes understanding and communication more complex than with black teas, yet the somewhat arbitrary Chinese naming convention reinforces the ancient romance and history of tea in its thousands of years of use within the country. There are hundreds, if not thousands, of unique tea names within China and Taiwan.

CHUN-MEE Harder twisted leaves.

GUNPOWDER Tightly rolled pinhead pellets.

HYSON An older, coarser tea leaf.

SOWMEE Small twisted leaves, similar to black broken grades.

YOUNG HYSON Young leaves made into long, wiry, thin leaf styles.

TEA TERMS & JARGON

BREW/INFUSIONS/LIQUOR These terms are synonymous and refer to the liquid tea during steeping and after the removal of the tea leaves.

CUPPA British slang meaning a cup of tea. Tea scholar James Norwood Pratt urges people to avoid use of this expression as he considers it "vulgar." Millions of British tea lovers may not concur.

CUPPING The practice of assessing tea by brewing, smelling, tasting, and critically analyzing a given sample.

HERBALS Herbal teas are made from an assortment of herbs, spices, flowers, fruits, and other botanicals, but not the tea plant *Camellia sinensis*. Although they do not contain tea, the term "herbal tea" has become commonplace in recent decades.

OFFERINGS Various tea samples presented for the purpose of assessment or cupping. A tea-trade term sometimes used by merchants when communicating with their customers.

ORIGIN A geographic region specific to where a type of tea is grown and processed.

SPECIALTY TEA This term embraces all varieties and different types of better-quality teas including longer-leaf styles, organic, and naturally flavored teas, as well as high-quality tea sachets (bags), and many single origin teas.

Buying & Storing Tea

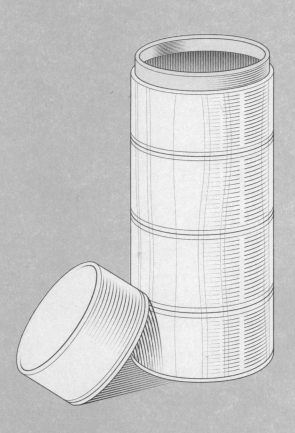

BUYING TEA

Now that you are familiar with the basic tea types, the next step is to select a tea for your own pleasure. There may be dozens or hundreds of options in a tea shop—even more when shopping online—but, like searching for a special wine, seasoning, or cooking oil, much of the adventure is in the selection process itself.

Buying tea can be an overwhelming experience. There are many thousands of tea vendors worldwide from online websites to brick-and-mortar retail tea shops. Where possible, buy tea first from a reputable tea merchant that you can visit. You can see, feel, and smell the tea before you decide which one you would like. Some tea shops will let you taste the tea before you make a purchase. Use your merchant's expertise and discuss with him or her the type of tea you wish to find.

When buying tea online, selection is much trickier, as the ability to smell, touch, and taste before purchase is missing, but either method becomes easier over time as you home in on what you like. One more concern is availability; inevitably, some of your favorites will be out of stock periodically. Subtle, never-ending shifts in flavor—influenced by variables in weather during the tea-growing cycle, processing, and other factors—also make stocking your tea inventory a little more complex. Buy less of a given tea until you know what you like and find satisfaction with a particular vendor.

A TIMELINE FOR TEA

Caffeine content aside, all teas can be enjoyed virtually anytime, yet a few seem ideally suited for certain times of the day or evening.

MORNING The stronger, single origin black teas from Assam, Ceylon, and China, as well as English and Irish breakfast blends, can help make greeting the day a little easier. These are sometimes best with a splash of cream or milk.

LUNCH/EARLY AFTERNOON Try mellower green teas (sencha, jasmine, matcha, Mao Feng) and oolong teas (Ali Shan, Bai Hao), which better suit the pace of a day already in gear.

DINNER/EARLY EVENING Oolongs, whites (Silver Needle, White Peony), and decaffeinated tea go well with dinner. For heartier meals, pu-erh is a tea of choice (it is reputed to help cut cholesterol and the bloat of fatty foods). White tea (served with fruit), or a limited edition, first flush tea (spring harvest) can dress up a fancier meal occasion.

BEDTIME Most people look for something with no caffeine at the end of the waking day. Herbal or fruit teas are caffeine-free and provide a soothing alternative.

CAFFEINE LEVELS IN TEA AND COFFEE

BREWED BEVERAGE	SERVING SIZE	CAFFEINE CONTENT RANGE
Black tea	8 oz (237 ml)	25–60 mg
Black tea, decaffeinated	8 oz (237 ml)	0–12 mg
Green tea	8 oz (237 ml)	25–50 mg
Brewed coffee (drip style)	8 oz (237 ml)	95–200 mg
Espresso (restaurant style)	1 oz (30 ml)	47–75 mg

SELECTING TEA

Arm yourself with a few key questions each time you buy tea to improve the effectiveness of the selection process.

IS CAFFEINE A CONCERN? If yes, head for herbal teas or decaffeinated teas (these contain only residual caffeine traces).

DO YOU LIKE TO START THE DAY WITH A FULL-BODIED, BRISK TEA? If yes, try a single origin Assam, Ceylon, or Chinese Keemun. Alternatively, try a blend of black teas such as provided in English or Irish breakfast teas.

DO YOU PREFER A LIGHTER CUP OF BLACK OR OOLONG TEA WITH EXCEPTIONAL CHARACTER? If yes, try a single estate origin Darjeeling, or a milder Ceylon or Indian Nilgiri tea.

WOULD YOU LIKE TO EXPLORE THE WORLD OF GREEN TEA, BUT ARE NOT SURE WHERE TO START? Try a medium-priced Japanese sencha (Japan's number-one green tea offering) or a Chinese green Mao Feng (the most popular green tea in China). Remember to brew lightly at first. Green tea laced with lemongrass, ginger, or peppermint adds nice variety to the green tea mix.

IS A SCENTED OR FLAVORED TEA OF INTEREST? Whether as a gift, or to add variety to your own exploration, seek out a jasmine green or perhaps a naturally flavored fruit tea—passion fruit, mango, or citrus—with a base of black tea.

THE TEA FLAVOR WHEEL

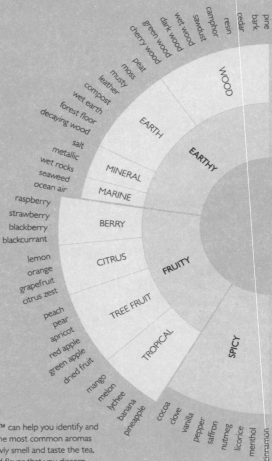

pine
bark
cedar
resin
camphor
sawdust
wet wood
dark wood
green wood
cherry wood
peat
moss
musty
leather
compost
wet earth
forest floor
decaying wood
salt
metallic
wet rocks
seaweed
ocean air
raspberry
strawberry
blackberry
blackcurrant
lemon
orange
grapefruit
citrus zest
peach
pear
apricot
red apple
green apple
dried fruit
mango
melon
lychee
banana
pineapple
cocoa
clove
vanilla
pepper
saffron
nutmeg
licorice
menthol
cinnamon

WOOD
EARTH
MINERAL
MARINE
BERRY
CITRUS
TREE FRUIT
TROPICAL

EARTHY
FRUITY
SPICY

The Tea Flavor Wheel™ can help you identify and
characterize some of the most common aromas
and flavors in tea.* Slowly smell and taste the tea,
and for each aroma and flavor that you discern,
start with the general category in the inner ring,
then move outward until you identify analogous
aroma or flavor in the outer ring.

* true tea, the infusion of the *Camellia sinensis* plant, not
other herbal infusions

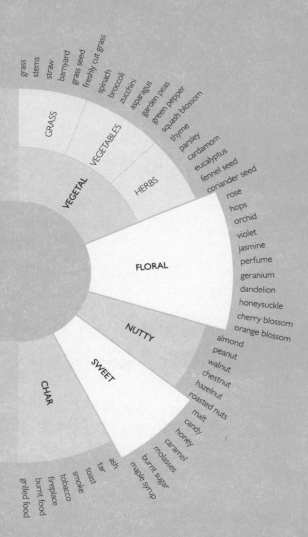

grass
stems
straw
barnyard
grass seed
freshly cut grass
spinach
broccoli
zucchini
asparagus
garden peas
green pepper
squash blossom
thyme
parsley
cardamom
eucalyptus
fennel seed
coriander seed
rose
hops
orchid
violet
jasmine
perfume
geranium
dandelion
honeysuckle
cherry blossom
orange blossom
almond
peanut
walnut
chestnut
hazelnut
roasted nuts
malt
candy
honey
caramel
burnt sugar
molasses
maple syrup
tar
ash
toast
smoke
tobacco
fireplace
burnt food
grilled food

GRASS
VEGETABLES
HERBS
VEGETAL
FLORAL
NUTTY
SWEET
CHAR

Graphic © copyright 2009 Christopher Gronbeck

BUYING GUIDE

Common sense and a few guidelines will help ensure that the products you select represent the best available tea. Quality, packaging, and contamination are the major targets; a little advance knowledge can help avoid potential problems.

QUALITY

Whether you visit a tea merchant in person or purchase tea by mail order from a catalogue or online, quality control on the part of the merchant is appropriate to ensure value. Of course, purchasing in person from a brick-and-mortar establishment makes checking the quality of your tea purchases somewhat easier, although some tea sellers do not allow some or all of the quality checks recommended below. Be assertive and purchase your tea with merchants that provide the most service, free or low-cost samples, and product information. There are simply too many great places to buy tea; there is no need to stick with less-than-supportive outlets.

Online websites selling tea should list a physical address and at the least a phone number. If not, do not shop there. Why? Not only will communication be limited to email, but also many sites operating like this are simply fronts that typically reroute your order to a master dealer, making a commission on every visitor. At this point, no one knows what level of quality control exists at such sellers.

Tea is a food and demands respect when it comes to quality. Additionally, the more ambiguous, hard-to-trace tea outlets may have slow or low volume and "sit" on tea inventories for months or years past their freshness expiration threshold. If a smaller or newer website wants your business, request they send you their names, media coverage they may have had recently, and awards or other affiliations that prove they are not rerouting your order to low-quality fulfillment centers.

The old adage "you get what you pay for" generally applies to finer specialty teas, but as with all consumer products, special deals, discounts, and incentives may also be obtained when shopping for tea. You should expect to receive discounts when you purchase large volumes. Depending upon the merchant, this may be at 4 or 8 ounces (about 115 or 230 grams) and then in pound or kilo quantities. Just as with fine wines and cheeses, pricing is not a guarantee of quality. Teas sold at a modest price can sometimes produce better brews than products sold for much more—yet another reason to learn the art of cupping and log your findings into a tea journal.

LOOSE TEA

Loose specialty tea presents tremendous economic value to consumers because there are between 100 to 250 cups of tea obtainable from each pound (0.45 kg), an effective increase over tea bags. Some of the long leaf, single origin teas can be brewed multiple times, further lowering the per-cup cost. What might look at first like a pricey "can't afford it" tea may cost far less than a dollar a cup! Compare that to coffee, which yields fifty plus servings per pound (0.45 kg), or energy drinks and even carbonated soda. Tea affords a healthy, delicious, daily beverage break at a cost no other beverage—besides water, and not the bottled variety—can match.

SERVINGS PER POUND (0.45 KG)

Loose-leaf green tea	125–250 servings	Brewed coffee	40–50 servings
Loose-leaf black tea	100–200 servings	Espresso coffee	60–65 servings

Sources: Tea Association of the USA, Teavana, Specialty Coffee Association of America

DIFFERENTLY SHAPED TEA BAGS

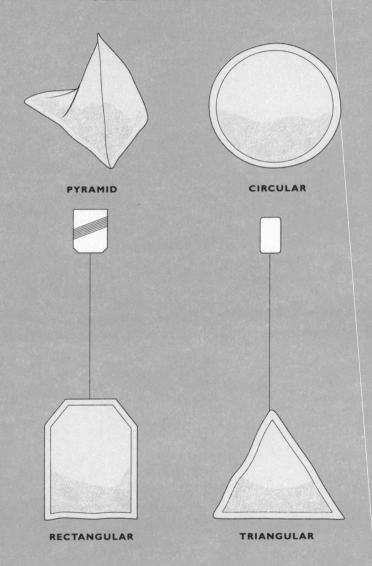

PYRAMID

CIRCULAR

RECTANGULAR

TRIANGULAR

When visiting a tea shop, ask the clerk if you can examine a specific tea or teas. Better outlets will either hand you a canister or sprinkle a little dry tea in your palm. If you have samples from a mail order merchant, conduct a tasting for each tea and decide what you like. Keep in mind that a specific tea from a select origin may or may not be the same with every purchase over time due to multiple variables. Tea is a natural product and weather, soil conditions, and other factors will periodically shift its sensory attributes, sometimes for the better, but not always.

Visually inspect the dry tea leaves. Are they consistent in shape and size—not perfectly, but overall—or are there radically different shapes, sizes, or even leaves that seem out of character with the others? Smell the dry tea leaf. Does it smell nice, like other similar samples, or is there no smell at all (not good and a sign of old tea)? Also be wary of off-odors; tea picks up other aromas easily and improperly stored tea means poor quality. Roll it around in your hand, gently crushing the leaves. Are they nicely pliable or do they break easily, leaving some dust (another sign of older tea)? Smelling the dry tea subsequent to a little handling will release fragrant oils, allowing for a greater examination of leaf character. Do not put your face into the tea container, but rather shake it a bit and let the escaping scent waft closely to your nose.

Taste the tea. Savvy tea merchants enjoy brewing tea for customers. Merchants that do not care to brew tea samples should have some system to allow you to take home samples for assessment. Some merchants offer this service for a nominal fee. Buy pricier teas in small quantities until you are confident that they are worth your money.

TEA BAGS

The use of larger tea bags has improved cup quality in recent years. New tea bag designs include pyramid shapes and large squares, larger size sachets that allow tea leaves to expand more fully, releasing more volatile flavor oils into the infusion. Even if you appreciate loose-leaf teas, tea bags are a more convenient option when traveling or brewing at the office.

COUNTERFEITS

While counterfeits are not much of a problem currently, there are exceptions when it comes to the issue of quality teas that are fakes, or simply diluted with inferior teas. This has become a specific issue with Darjeeling teas. As the demand for these teas outpaces supply in some years, insiders in the tea trade have noted that some stocks of supposedly pure Darjeeling tea have been diluted with cheaper teas from southern India, or, more commonly, Nepalese teas, which have a strikingly similar taste profile to the Darjeelings. Even skilled tea masters can have a tough time discerning improprieties in these adulterated products. By keeping a small amount of your favorite teas on hand, it is easy to compare quality from season to season. If your favorite tea tastes, looks, and smells strangely different from the same tea from previous years, bring it to your merchant's attention.

Pu-erh tea has increasingly been subject to artificial aging, counterfeit labels, and worse. Real pu-erh tea commands an ultra-premium price in the world marketplace, with pressure from collectors who pay top dollar for aged cakes when they are decades old or older. Unscrupulous merchants have learned how to quite deftly press newer teas into the classic round cakes that distinguish pu-erh, add various compounds to change aromas and colors, and wrap them in counterfeit labels, much the same way as counterfeit watches and other fashion accessories are forged. There is little one can do to bypass these ersatz pu-erh teas, short of knowing the origin tea garden, manufacturer, or reliable reseller. Like all tea, building and maintaining strong relationships with pu-erh merchants of good repute helps prevent the purchase of fakes. Repetitive tasting of pu-erh helps as well, but there is no foolproof guard against this kind of insidious and growing tea crime.

CONTAMINANTS

Tea, like any other food or beverage, runs the risk of contamination from a variety of substances including agricultural chemicals such as pesticides and herbicides, and naturally occurring contaminants such as heavy metals. Improved quality-control systems that are implemented at the producing estate or farm reduce some issues, yet others remain. Overall, tea is a safe beverage, yet there are a few points you should be aware of when it comes to purity.

One way to improve tea purity is by purchasing certified organic teas. Such teas will be free from pesticides, herbicides, and other noxious, synthetic chemical agents—though trace levels may still be present. Note that old-timer tea experts commonly scoff at the cup quality of brewed organic teas, noting they simply do not taste as good as their conventional counterparts. Sadly, this position is sometimes accurate.

PESTICIDES

Tea plants have the same insect, mold, and other problems that plague many other agricultural crops worldwide, as well as some that are unique to the species. In response, the use of pesticides, herbicides, and anti-fungal agents is common in most tea-growing regions. Many of these chemicals are hazardous, yet advocates of traditional farming methods that employ such substances proclaim that little residue transfers to the dried leaves or into brewed tea infusions.

Scientific study has not delved deeply into this area so far, helping fuel a skeptical consumer base that has made certified organic teas as popular as their equivalents in vegetables, fruits, and coffee. It is a tough issue for conventional tea farmers to face, especially those who would like to avoid such chemicals but have not found ways to transition their crops to organic production. Some artisan tea merchants promote the idea that smaller tea farmers in many parts of the world do not use chemical agents simply because they cannot afford them.

This is true in some cases and is not a universal practice. The only way to securely bypass the presence of synthetic chemicals in your tea is by purchasing certified organic teas.

HEAVY METALS & PATHOGENS

All plants absorb not only beneficial but also toxic constituents—these include heavy metals such as aluminum, zinc, and lead—from both ground water and the soil. In heavily polluted areas, even rainfall can carry toxic elements. Local power plants (not uncommon in China and parts of India) and automobile emissions produce pollution that is picked up by the rainfall, which both nurtures tea plants and may simultaneously shower them with undesirable elements. Some of these toxic substances are also transferred from soil to the plant itself as it grows.

Accumulation of heavy metals in major tea-producing regions such as China and India is an increasing long-term health concern, and there is intensely concentrated pollution in some premier tea-growing areas. However, few tea producers test their teas for metal content. Organic teas are typically tested in independent laboratories, not only for pesticide levels, but also metal content. Those with high levels are rejected. The EU has the strictest quality control standards for tea anywhere in the world. Teas imported from the EU are also likely to be purer; organic teas from the EU are among the purest available from an overall purity perspective.

Dangerous pathogens such as *E. coli*, *Salmonella*, and strains of harmful yeast and mold have rarely been a problem for teas worldwide. Better producers and brands routinely test for them, in any case. If detected, the presence of *E. coli* or *Salmonella* would prevent a given tea from entering commerce—though slip-ups can occur. Teas marked by overly abundant yeast and mold levels do make it into the market on occasion. Using water that has reached a boil is optimal for safety concerns in this realm of tea product purity.

THE ART OF STORING TEA

Storing and keeping tea as fresh as possible for both daily use and the longer term is quite simple and only involves a few basic policies and procedures. As so often occurs with spices, coffee, and many other provisions, well-meaning consumers purchase quality tea but then improperly store it, with negative outcomes that could easily be avoided. One would not dare buy a fine wine, uncork it, and leave it uncorked for days or weeks—exposed to air and odor—and then expect the same delicious freshness as when it was first opened. Tea is the same. It simply cannot be left out or open, exposed to the atmospheric elements of a kitchen or pantry, and then be expected to perform well in the teapot and cup.

Some loose teas, particularly bulk dried leaves, are packaged by merchandizers in resealable, impermeable bags, but more often they are simply placed in thin paper bags with a little twist-tie at the top. Leaving a couple of ounces of loose tea in such a bag and then consuming it out of this unit is fine for short-term enjoyment, but it is not an optimal situation. To fully protect your investment in great quality tea, it should be transferred to suitable containers once it arrives home. These containers—and where they are placed—largely determine how long the tea will retain its character and freshness.

The chief enemies of stored tea are moisture, heat, light, and aromas. Moisture, primarily from humidity, can vary in threat level depending on your geographic location and time of year, and is countered with standard moisture-proof containers—glass, stainless steel, plastic, or ceramic—with tight-sealing lids. The danger from moisture is compounded with tea because it is hygroscopic, rapidly absorbing moisture from the air. In most kitchens, moist air also carries with it a melange of aromas that will come to rest on your tea. When infused into the cup, this is rarely a pleasant experience. Highly flavored or scented teas, especially Lapsang Souchong, should be very carefully stored apart from other teas, as their signature aromas can also generate smells that will easily contaminate other, more delicate teas.

Heat degrades tea by speeding up the deterioration of its key flavor and nutritional constituents. Normal room temperature may be suitable for tea in many geographic zones and regulated indoor living conditions, but anything over 80°F (27°C) is unsuitable for prolonged storage. In most kitchens, the biggest heat threat comes from ovens and stovetops; store tea away from these appliances.

Light is also a threat, from either sunlight or artificial sources, but the latter is by far the most dangerous. As with heat, various containers will provide appropriate protection, including those made from opaque glass, stainless steel, plastic, and ceramics. Kitchens are a primary source of odors in the home, and these emanations—even if they smell good, as from cooking, spices, or brewing coffee—are not a friend to tea. Tightly sealed containers are once again the solution.

Loose tea should be transferred from the packaging in which it was shipped or purchased to an appropriate container. The lids for tea containers must fit snugly. Some people drop the entire package their tea arrives in directly into a designated caddy. These tea containers provide the best protection when stored in a cupboard away from everything else and never next to spices, coffee, or food.

Never store tea in the freezer or refrigerator. While low temperatures are considered by some to prolong freshness in tea (and other dried commodities), this potential advantage is offset by the high moisture content inside, not to mention multiple sources of odors. Moisture and odors will individually or together ruin tea, often even when it is apparently stored safely inside sealed containers. Only high-end teas stored under the guidance of tea masters are kept in cold conditions, and these are housed in specially sealed packages under strictly controlled conditions.

Some ultra-rare and single origin, limited-harvest teas are placed in foil packages and then nitrogen-flushed to remove most of the oxygen. It is oxygen that is the enemy of freshness for tea, because it is the major component required to fuel the process of decay.

TEA CONTAINERS

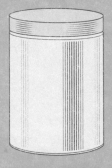

STAINLESS STEEL

OPAQUE GLASS

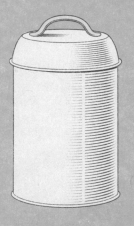

PLASTIC

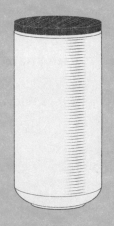

CERAMIC

Suitable containers for tea can be made from
stainless steel, opaque glass, plastic, and ceramics.

Nitrogen-flushed foil packs are essentially hermetically sealed units and may be stored as is or unopened, inside a large canister or jar as well. Many of these sealed foil bags also contain a desiccant pack—a small pouch the size of an eraser that absorbs moisture out of the air. Desiccant packs do help to neutralize any moisture that may seep into packages, and they can even trap moisture as it escapes from fresh tea leaves. The desiccant packs should be tossed once the tea from a given unit is finished; avoid having them drop into teapots or brewing appliances and keep them away from pets and children.

When tea is past its prime, it simply goes flat. There is little flavor, minimal aroma, and perhaps a lighter color in the brewed infusion. Old tea leaves are also brittle. These results come from the evaporation of the essential volatile oils within the tea leaves. Despite the flatness, however, "dead" tea is not dangerous. A small handful of teas may ripen and improve over time, including some pu-erh, Keemun, and darker oolongs.

WHAT IS THE SHELF LIFE OF TEA?

Tea blend masters and merchants often debate about how long loose tea may be kept before it is essentially devoid of flavor and aroma. Assuming the tea has been stored properly, there are general guidelines that vary for different tea types. Gunpowder green tea, with its tightly rolled balls or pellets, may be tasty for up to three years. Some Chinese Keemun tea and very tightly rolled oolongs stored in nitrogen-flushed foil bags (with desiccant packs) can last up to a few years and still retain most of their character. Store pu-erh in a cool, dark space, by itself, on a shelf where air can circulate around it. Experts suggest leaving it in the paper wrapper it arrives in, as well as using a larger outer bag to protect it from dust and unwanted aromas. The chart opposite shows the average freshness life of tea when properly stored.

THE AVERAGE FRESHNESS LIFE OF TEA

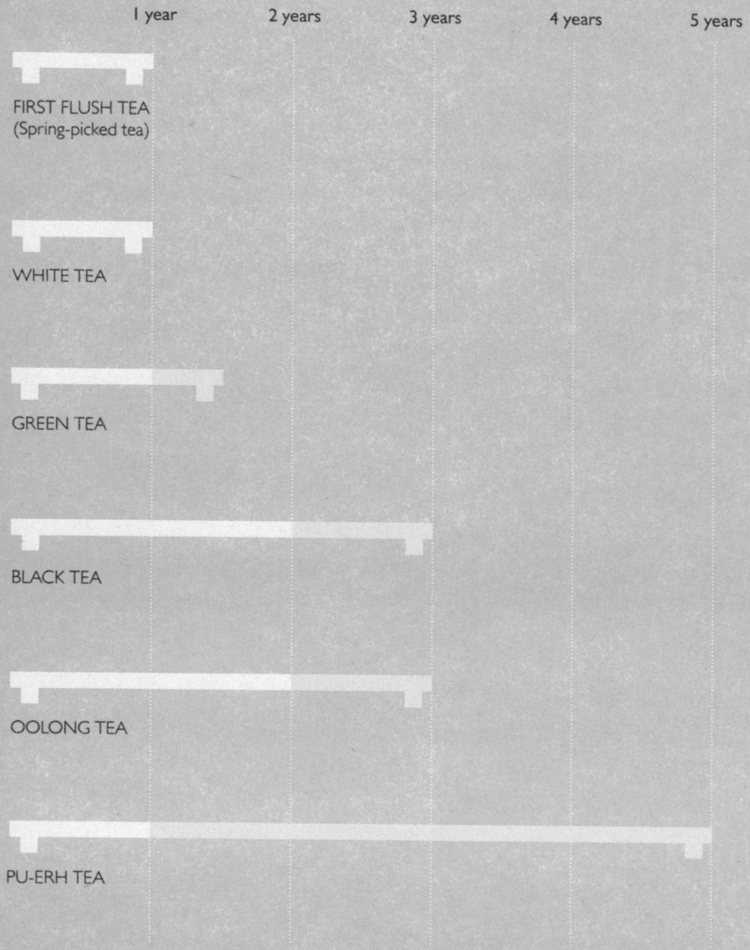

	1 year	2 years	3 years	4 years	5 years

FIRST FLUSH TEA
(Spring-picked tea)

WHITE TEA

GREEN TEA

BLACK TEA

OOLONG TEA

PU-ERH TEA

The Basic Necessities

WATER FOR TEA

There are several ways in which your tea-drinking experience can be enhanced. These include improving water quality, understanding the quantity of tea to be used per serving, learning brewing techniques, selecting condiments, and determining which teas go well with food. Some tea experts suggest that the use of good-quality water can make the difference between a great cup of tea and a mediocre one.

Good-quality water is so intrinsic to making great tea that in China there is an old proverb: "Water is the mother of tea." No serious tea lover will disagree, but many tea drinkers have yet to explore this commodity as a key component of brewing satisfaction.

With few exceptions worldwide, tap water is full of chlorine. This is used to purify and balance the mineral content of municipal water supplies, and experts consider it to be the primary destroyer of tea quality. While the presence of some minerals can add flavor, tap water can contain too many minerals, or in some cases, hold quantities of dangerous metals such as lead. One or more of these undesirable elements are common in the majority of household water supplies and can have a heavy and detrimental impact on the taste of tea brewed with water obtained from domestic or industrial sources. These components can distort tea in every way: flavor, aroma, and color. In spite of this fact, many people brew their tea with tap water, and never experience the amazing improvement in taste that better-quality water can make.

THE PH SCALE

The pH scale (representing the activity of hydrogen ions) is widely used to measure the acidity or alkalinity of substances, with a range from 0 to 14. A pH level of 7 represents neutral; numbers below 7 indicate acidity and those above, alkalinity (base).

Pure water is neutral, with a pH of 7; some tap and spring waters register at this level, but most do not.[1] The best tea is brewed with water that is either pH neutral (7) or slightly acidic (6.5–6.9), indicating the presence of some minerals.

Some tea aficionados spend inordinate amounts of time and money assessing and manipulating the pH of their tea water, but the ultimate, easiest, and most affordable way to test water quality is by making a pot of tea with tap water and the same with a small amount of pure bottled spring water, often called "artesian." If you can't taste the difference, don't change the water source.

The ultimate way to check water for chlorine and mineral content is through testing. Both commercial and over-the-counter test kits provide information for consumers who need to know this information. But for thousands of years, people have relied upon their tongues and noses to determine water quality. The simple rule of thumb: poor-quality water smells "off." If you question your own water supply, try a few alternatives and use your own senses to see if your tea will benefit.

FILTERED WATER

Water filters provide consistent, high-quality water for tea. They are widely available, with affordable models ranging from simple faucet attachments to self-filtering pitchers. Whole-house water filters are also increasingly in use. All of these units typically use disposable cartridges that rely on activated charcoal to remove chlorine, some minerals, and other contaminants. They can provide dozens—even hundreds—of gallons of water before the filter needs to be replaced.

More expensive units rely on reverse osmosis, ceramic filters, or ultraviolet light to purify water, and most effectively remove biological contaminants, but provide no added advantage for taste. With water filters used for tea, chlorine is the main target for removal.

[1] The USGS Water Science School. United States Geological Survey.

FAUCET FILTER

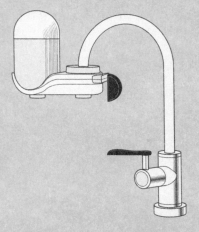

Replaceable filter cartridges are the
heart of these point-of-use devices, which attach
directly to kitchen faucets.

WATER FILTER PITCHER

These basic units use disposable filter
cartridges that effectively remove chlorine
and other unwanted elements.

TAP WATER

If you use tap water for brewing tea, run the faucet for a couple of minutes if it has not been used overnight. This lessens the potential for accumulations of chlorine and other unwelcome compounds. Run the faucet each morning using cold water, not hot. Hot water has been deaerated by virtue of sitting within a hot-water heater, making it dull, flat, and lifeless. Once the tap has run cold for a couple of minutes, fill your kettle. If you have the time and patience, fill a pitcher or other container with cold water from the tap and let it sit overnight before using—almost all of the chlorine in the tap water will dissipate naturally.

DISTILLED WATER

Distilled water is often sought after as a cleaner, safer alternative to tap water. However, because all of the minerals have been removed from distilled water—and some mineral content adds desirable flavor to water—this option is not ideal for tea. Tea made with distilled water is exceptionally dull and flat, with no brightness or sparkle in the cup. In most cases, tap water is preferable to distilled water for making tea, when no other options are available.

SPRING WATER

Many types of bottled water use natural spring water. If you live within a major metropolitan area it will be rare to find such water from the tap. However, water pumped from underground basins or collected from artesian wells is a source of drinking water for many rural households. Some well and spring water is simply too heavy in mineral content to make good tea; it causes brewed tea to taste chalk-like and ruins complex flavors and aromas. On the other hand, this type of water source may also have a perfect natural balance of minerals and oxygen, making for great tea. The only way to know for sure is to compare, using filtered alternatives and outside sources as benchmarks.

Tea aficionados banter and debate endlessly about how much tea to use when brewing a cup or pot. There is both art and science involved in this decision, but it comes down to personal preference and little else. While connoisseurs and tea masters may debate and profess universal standards for the correct ratio of dry tea to water, reality suggests this should be considered a guideline rather than a rule. There are three ways in which one can determine how much tea should be dropped into a teapot or cup: use a teaspoon, rely on "eyeballing" with the pinch method, or utilize a small scale.

The strength and intensity of brewed tea, as it relates to the amount of dry tea used, is a matter of trial and error in order to ultimately deliver the brew that is most satisfying. The ratio of water to tea that you settle on is also subject to change; not only does each teapot and cup hold varying amounts of liquid, but most teas undergo flavor shifts seasonally, meaning the amount of tea needed may vary slightly from year to year.

SPOONS

The universally used teaspoon measuring device used in cooking may serve the purpose for consistency in measuring; however, common tableware teaspoons vary tremendously in capacity. The amount of tea a non-standardized teaspoon might hold can vary by over a gram or even more, enough to radically alter the final brew.

Therefore, when using a teaspoon a little trial and error is required to determine how many units of a specific tea are ideal for brewing either a cupful or a teapot. Once determined, use the same spoon for all tea measuring, and note how the tea leaves fill the spoon—less than level, level, rounded, or heaped—and make this your benchmark.

DIGITAL TEA SCALE

This device is portable and runs
on batteries. Good for tea or spices. It is accurate
to a fraction of a gram or ounce.

CLASSIC MECHANICAL SCALE

The go-to standard for hundreds of years,
this type of scale is still in wide use. It may require a little
practice and patience for effective use.

THE PINCH

The technique that is most handy for measuring tea for final use is your own hand, using the pinch method. This is the preferred method used by tea lovers in many countries because of its convenience, but it may make the novice tea brewer a little nervous. Just how much is in a pinch? Traditionally, some cookbooks once defined a pinch (the amount of an ingredient that can be held between the forefinger and thumb, sometimes using the middle finger as well), as ⅛ teaspoon; other sources refer to this amount as a "dash," and a pinch as ¹⁄₁₆ teaspoon.[2]

Tea, however, unlike salt, baking powder, or other granular food ingredients, varies considerably in volume; some types feature large whole leaves, others broken leaves, rolled leaves, or leaf particles. To be consistent, the pinch method has to follow the same guideline as with teaspoons: use your eye and the tactile feedback from your fingers to set a benchmark. With practice, a single pinch can routinely provide the ideal amount of tea. As a rule of thumb, use a larger pinch—or multiple pinches—for large-leafed teas and a smaller pinch for smaller, denser teas.

SCALES

The amount of dry tea needed is most accurately determined by weight rather than volume, because the many types of tea vary considerably in their dried forms. Therefore, weighing is the most reliable method of determining the right amount of tea and a small scale is the right tool for this job. A digital pocket scale that can measure in 0.01 ounce (0.1 gram) increments is ideal for use at home.

Scales are most often used by professional tea tasters. But occasionally pulling out a scale at home will help you learn how much tea really is in that favorite teaspoon, or how much a pinch of your favorite tea actually weighs.

[2] *A Dictionary of Units of Measurements.* Russ Rowlett, University of North Carolina. 2005.

HOW MUCH TEA TO USE PER CUP

A standard cup or mug has a capacity of 6 to 8 fluid ounces (180 to 240 ml). Traditional teacups, including those with matching saucers, are usually smaller, holding 4 to 6 fluid ounces (120 to 180 ml). For most teas enjoyed in the West, one teaspoon of tea (2 to 3 grams) per cup of water provides the proper amount.

For many longer-leaf teas, more common in the Eastern hemisphere, the weight is more commonly 3 to 4 grams of tea per cup of water. Tea quantities are therefore smaller for traditional teacups than for mugs.

Smaller leaf styles and many black teas may only require one level teaspoon per cup, whereas longer-leafed teas benefit from more—a rounded teaspoonful.

Tightly curled balls of tea, such as some oolongs, jasmine pearls, and gunpowder greens, also only need a teaspoon or even less per cup. These varieties unfurl during brewing; as the leaves expand, much of their flavor is released.

Smoky or very dense (small leaf) teas, and many flavored teas, may only require one teaspoon per two cups.

HOW MUCH TEA TO USE IN TEAPOTS

Teapots vary in size; a standard size is 32 fluid ounces (960 ml). So, an average pot of tea may require four to six teaspoons of tea (8 to 12 grams). Some traditional Chinese teapots may only hold 5 to 6 fluid ounces (150 to 180 ml) and may require less or more tea depending on the type used.

Carefully measure your water quantities for either teapots or cups and keep the quantities consistent. Vary the amount of tea rather than the water to establish the ratio that is ideal for you. Larger infusers require less tea because their larger volumes allow more water to circulate with the tea.

WATER TEMPERATURES

Proper water temperature is another important part of the process of brewing good tea. Many people will purchase great tea and a flashy kettle, carefully measure the amount of tea per serving, and choose an appropriate source of water, but then pay scant attention to water temperatures.

How much tea to use and how long to steep it are relatively subjective decisions, though some core guidelines are helpful. However, proper water temperatures in the broader tea categories—black, green, and oolong—are objective and apply universally. The process of applying water at the right temperature allows just the right amount of aromatic compounds, tannins, astringent polyphenols (antioxidants), and amino acids to be flushed from the leaves and grace your teapot or cup with sensory and cerebral satisfaction.

Once water has reached the temperature of a full boil, most of the oxygen in the water is released. Oxygen plays a key role in bringing out the taste of tea by helping the aromatic compounds—mostly the volatile oils in the leaves—transfer to a gaseous state, which also yields scent, a sensory agent closely allied with taste.

The goal when boiling water for black and most oolong teas is to let the kettle reach a boil and then immediately pour it over the tea leaves, never allowing the kettle to continue boiling for more than a few seconds. A prolonged period of boiling eventually "flattens" the water through distillation. Water that boils too long tends to be dull and lifeless, something to be avoided.

Water that has been allowed to cool too long will also inhibit optimum tea brewing. But for highly scented and flavored teas, such as black, green, and oolong categories, tastier brews may be produced if slightly cooler water is used than for their unflavored, unscented counterparts.

IDEAL TEMPERATURES

At sea level, water boils at 212°F (100°C); as altitudes increase it boils at lesser temperatures. For example, at 1,000 feet (305 m), the boiling point is 210°F (99°C) and at 2,000 feet (610 m), it boils at 208°F (98°C). When brewing tea, aim for the desired temperature.

BLACK TEAS At 195 to 212°F (90 to 100°C), water should reach, or nearly reach, a full boil, then be immediately stopped and poured over the tea leaves. Do not let the kettle boil furiously; over-heated water is not ideal for black teas. But, water that is too cool will not extract all of the oils and other elements that produce a robust, strong cup of tea. Pouring from a kettle that has boiled for a few minutes or using water that is simply not warm enough will produce weak, tepid black tea.

OOLONG TEAS These complex teas run the gamut from lightly oxidized (like strong green teas) to almost fully oxidized (closer to a black tea profile) and flexibility is needed when targeting water temperatures. Cooler water for lighter oolongs is recommended; temperature should not exceed 180 to 185°F (82 to 85°C), and hotter water (close to boiling) for darker (black to dark-green) oolong teas.

GREEN TEAS Water that has barely reached a full boil and then cooled a couple of minutes is ideal for green teas, which are quite sensitive to extreme water temperatures. Using water that is too hot to brew green teas results in bitter tea. The target is 160 to 185°F (71 to 85°C). Some ultra-delicate first flush Japanese and Chinese green teas may taste better with even cooler water: 150 to 160°F (65 to 71°C).

WHITE TEAS Some tea connoisseurs suggest that white teas be brewed with water temperatures in the same range as that used for green teas. But, white teas do not get bitter when exposed to extremely hot water, as green teas often do, and hotter water can be used. The target range is 185 to 200°F (85 to 93°C).

THERMOMETERS

Small pocket-size thermometers are handy for
testing water temperatures. Even occasional use will help you
learn when the water in your kettle has reached
the ideal temperature.

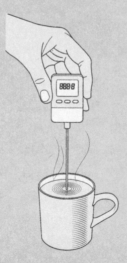

Modern digital thermometers are preferable,
as they can give almost instant readings.

CAFÉ STYLE KETTLE

A countertop appliance provides hot water on
demand. Internal reservoirs hold enough water for family or
office use, boiling and dispensing individual servings
quickly (typically in 1 to 2 minutes).

ELECTRIC WATER KETTLE

Electric kettles are an efficient way to heat water
directly. Most turn off automatically when the water reaches the
temperature to boil, or when they run out of water. Some advanced
designs feature multiple preset temperature settings,
ideal for different kinds of tea.

TEA BREWING

Once water has reached the proper temperature and been poured over the tea leaves, you are ready to time the brewing cycle. The length of the brewing cycle depends upon the type of tea and personal preference. The use of a timer is highly recommended.

Repeated studies have documented how consumers use tea bags, and the results demonstrate that people consistently underestimate how much time has passed. Many people remove tea bags from the cup in as little as 30 to 90 seconds, even when the recommended steeping time is 3 to 4 minutes. In fact, many people steep their tea according to color, not time, removing the tea leaves—whether it is in tea bags or in an infuser—as soon as the water darkens. Inevitably, under-brewed tea is weak and not satisfying; over-brewed tea is often bitter and too astringent. Timing is an important part of the successful tea-preparation matrix. Even expert tea brewers often over- or underestimate the amount of time that has passed as tea brews.

Whatever type of timer is used—from a traditional hourglass sand timer to a modern digital device—tea drinkers will quickly appreciate the substantial impact steeping time has when preparing tea. As with the guidelines for the ideal amount of tea to use per serving, the length of a brewing cycle for a teapot or individual cup of tea follows general rules, but personal preference has a role to play as well.

Some research indicates that once past 3 minutes of steeping time, the maximum levels of soluble matter (flavor and aroma compounds) have been extracted from the leaves. After 3 minutes, only additional tannins are released, increasing the strength of the brew, but not necessarily in a desirable manner when it comes to taste. In general, longer brew times are desirable for black teas and some oolongs, but never for green teas.

Some tea drinkers believe that most of the caffeine content in tea can be dissipated by rinsing the tea leaves with hot water—and discarding this rinse water—before brewing for a prescribed length of time.

Although most of the caffeine remains, this method does remove enough caffeine to benefit people who are overly sensitive. As a result of the rinse, some flavor and aroma is also lost along with caffeine.

In general, Chinese teas are a little more forgiving than their Japanese counterparts when steeped. That is, they tend not to be as astringent or bitter when brewed for long periods. This is partially due to the way in which the oxidative process is halted during processing certain teas. Chinese teas often use pan- or oven-firing methods during processing, compared to Japanese teas, in which steam treatments are more common. The difference affects how the teas respond to brewing times. Overall, Japanese teas—largely green tea types—require shorter steeping times than green teas from other regions.

STEEPING TIMES

BLACK TEA 3 to 6 minutes. If adding milk or cream after the leaves have been removed for a breakfast tea, strong Assam, or Ceylon tea, a longer steep time of 4 to 6 minutes helps the tea "stand up" boldly and briskly so that the flavor shines through even if condiments are added.

OOLONG TEA 3 to 5 minutes

GREEN TEA 1.5 to 3 minutes

WHITE TEA 4 to 6 minutes

When using high-quality, longer-leaf teas, the tea leaves will often yield a second, third, or even more brews from the original batch of leaves. The reuse of some tea leaves pays splendid dividends in terms of thriftiness, with minimal diminishment of flavor. However, subsequent brews of the same tea leaves require longer steeping times for each additional brew. Smaller-leaf styles and tea bags generally require less steeping time.

HOURGLASS TIMER

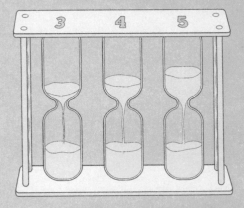

Old-fashioned, but effective, hourglass timers provide a
visual reference for ideal tea brewing. This unified design has three
separate time spans to accommodate different timings.

DIGITAL TIMER

Small, portable digital timers provide countdown timing for
perfect brews. Specialized units just for tea have preset, one-button
controls for common brewing preferences.

ONE-CUP TEA INFUSER

This is a contemporary single-cup infuser. The removable lid
stays in place during brewing and is removed when steeping is complete;
it neatly holds the infuser when it is removed from the cup.

TEA-BALL STYLE
LOOSE-TEA INFUSER

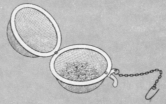

One of the most common types of infuser,
this device can be messy to use and is typically undersized,
restricting the expansion of the tea leaves during brewing.

OPEN LOOSE-TEA INFUSER

This classic, elegant-style tea strainer is effective when pouring
brewed tea from a teapot, and has plenty of room for the tea leaves
to expand and hot water to circulate.

TURBULENCE & BREWING

Under optimum conditions, tea leaves will expand two to five times their original size when immersed in hot water. When tea leaves cannot expand naturally during brewing, the end result is compromised. Most people who use loose tea for brewing rely on small "tea balls" —also called "tea eggs"—infusers that contain the tea while it is immersed in hot water. Most of these infusers are not large enough to allow the tea leaves to expand properly. Dunking these popular tea-brewing contraptions in and out of a cup or teapot can improve the results, but only slightly.

Traditionally, the natural expansion of tea leaves during brewing is known as "the agony of the leaves." It is a fascinating process to watch, especially in glass teapots and mugs, and is essential to the character of the final brew because of the tannins released and the volatile oils unleashed. Simultaneously, the water changes color. This wondrous alchemy transmutes the dried leaves of a simple plant into a dynamic liquid refreshment with exceedingly diverse properties. The full expansion of tea leaves during brewing is essential, and it can benefit from an action called turbulence.

Turbulence is the intentional movement of the tea leaves during the brewing process and can greatly enhance the final quality of the tea. This is a fascinating part of the tea-brewing process that is largely ignored, even by tea experts. However, laboratory evidence supports the value of turbulence in improving properties of brewed tea.[3]

Traditionally, tea leaves are placed into a teapot for later straining and decanting into a serving vessel, or individual cups. In most cases, the leaves are left to steep and unfurl on their own after hot water has been added; the addition of the water by itself adds some movement to the leaves. The results are universally acceptable; after all, this is how tea has been made for centuries. However, improvement is possible.

[3]Unpublished research from ChromaDex, Inc. (Irvine, CA).

Designers of modern tea-brewing equipment have introduced new high-tech equipment that incorporates turbulence into the brewing process through controlled, automated agitation. A little movement when brewing tea leaves optimizes the transfer of the desirable elements from the leaves into the brew.

You can employ some of the same action on your own, however, without relying on new brewing devices. When using a teapot, stir the tea leaves gently a few times after adding hot water. If the teapot has a built-in infuser basket, do the same by stirring the leaves inside the infuser, or if the infuser is a separate unit, dunk or spin it a few times while it is immersed. If an infuser basket is used with an individual teacup, do the same by gently lifting the infuser in and out of the cup a few times as tea begins to steep. In any use of infusers, use devices that are large enough to permit the full expansion of the tea leaves.

In smaller, ornate teacups and pots, a small spoon, or a chopstick can be used to stir the leaves a bit during brewing. Gentle movements are all that is needed; the turbulence desired does not require brisk or energetic action.

You may be surprised at how rich, full, and solid your tea brews are with some occasional, friendly agitation and movement of the tea leaves. An added bonus is slightly faster brewing times—even if this is not the main goal. Aside from better-tasting tea, the agitation of the tea also helps release more of the healthy polyphenols, antioxidants, and minerals from the leaves.

"Old school" tea lovers and practitioners of classic tea-brewing methods may scoff at the thought of agitating the leaves during the "agony of brewing leaves," as this is not part of the long-running tradition associated with this beverage. But new generations of tea fans seek every possible edge to enhance their tea-brewing experiences, and a little turbulence may provide one such advantage.

TEA THERMOS WITH INFUSER

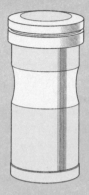

This portable container keeps the
tea hot and includes an infuser inside the top
for on-the-go tea brewing.

SMALL TEA THERMOS WITH INFUSER

A see-through portable container
is effective for brewing tea on the go, but
it can break if dropped.

CONDIMENTS

Many serious tea experts consider the addition of anything besides tea leaves and water to their beloved brews an abomination. This is especially the case in Asia, where green tea dominates, less so in the western world, where there is a long history of adding condiments to black tea. The addition of sweeteners, citrus, and milk to black teas started because poorer tea grades were often astringently bitter, and these condiments made the tea more palatable and offset overly intense flavors. The tradition of adding these extras to black teas first took hold in much of Great Britain and Europe; by the later 1800s and early 1900s, black tea was routinely served with sugar, cream, or milk, and occasionally, a wedge of lemon.

MILK & CREAM

The hard-and-fast rule with dairy-based additives is that they are only suitable for use in black tea. Stronger Indian (Assam and breakfast blends) and Ceylon teas may also work with these additives, but rarely do Chinese black or oolong teas unless these are part of hearty, brisk breakfast-style tea blends. Darjeeling—the "champagne of teas," and also a black tea—should never be doused with milk or cream.

Proteins found in milk and cream bind with select tannins (the bitter constituents found naturally in tea leaves), making them somewhat less pungent and astringent. The resulting brew is smoother, with a softer taste. Milk, and especially cream, also contributes to mouthfeel, the term used to describe textural feel of the liquid on the tongue and palate, generating a silkier sensation.

Science, but not all public opinion, declares that when using milk in tea, the milk should be added to the cup first, before the tea is added.

In the reverse—the milk is added to the hot tea—the proteins in the milk can be partially deactivated, reducing their ability to smooth out the astringency in the tea. Some suggest that by adding the milk first, there can be a tendency to add too much—an argument for adding the milk last. This disagreement has continued for more than a century. While the science supports the "milk first, tea second" approach, both techniques are acceptable; it's truly a matter of personal preference.

SUGAR

Common white table sugar—granulated or in cubes—is often served with black tea, especially in afternoon and high tea services. Like milk, sugar was first used to help reduce the bitterness in low-quality black teas from India and Ceylon, but the practice, once established, continued even when high-quality teas were widely available, due to the increasing affordability and availability of sugar.

Sugar is a common ingredient in chai tea served in India, now commonplace in North America. Chai is a blend of black tea, spices, and sugar. Sugar is also an ever-constant sweetener in Moroccan green mint tea, where it is used in heavy quantities, often many teaspoons per serving.

With chai the exception, a fine black tea from any origin simply does not need sugar to improve or enhance its natural flavor; sweeteners obscure the true quality of the tea. Green teas, increasingly part of the American beverage menu, are also best enjoyed without sweeteners. The exception for both green and black teas is iced tea, especially in ready-to-drink forms, where sugar or other sweeteners are the standard. "Sweet tea," the standard iced tea beverage in the southern states, is always served sweetened, though some restaurants offer the curiously termed option, "unsweetened sweet tea."

CITRUS

A small dash of citrus is another holdout from the cultural antiquity of tea. As with sugar, citrus and other condiments have been traditional accompaniments, masking the less-desirable properties of poor-quality teas. Citrus added to tea dramatically alters aroma and flavor, in most cases not desirably; even the natural color of brewed tea is negatively impacted. If citrus is added to tea when the milk has already been added, it will likely curdle, creating a horrific effect: off-putting flavor, confusing aromas, and cloudiness. If your preference is to add a splash of lemon or orange to your tea, add it after the tea is in the cup, and then, gingerly.

Interestingly, the world's most popular flavored and scented tea, Earl Grey, is essentially black tea with bergamot. Bergamot is a member of the citrus family and, in the case of Earl Grey, the addition of bergamot makes it an absolute delight for millions of people around the world who enjoy it daily.

HONEY

Honey is commonplace in kitchens around the world. It has long been used to sweeten black tea and even green tea on occasion. Honey has a surprisingly strong impact on tea flavor, and not always a positive one. It tends to dissipate, dominating the heady, aromatic notes of the better black teas; a simple white sugar has less impact and is a little more desirable if a sweetener must be used. If you do prefer honey, seek out mild clover honey and steer clear of the strong, dark varieties, which simply overwhelm even the strongest black teas.

STEVIA

Stevia is a common plant native to South America and Mexico. It is a non-caloric sweetener, 100 to 250 times sweeter than sucrose (common table sugar). There is a plentiful body of science-based research that has fully documented stevia's safety, and it is rapidly becoming the non-sugar favorite in major commercial brands of colas and sport beverages. Compared to sugar, stevia in its natural form has a curious, slightly hay-like flavor; some people detect a licorice-like taste. Powdered, refined extracts of stevia have a taste closer to sugar, and, to date, this natural sweetener has attracted none of the controversy linked to chemical sweeteners such as aspartame, sucralose, and saccharin. For those seeking an alternative to sugar for their tea or chai blend, stevia may be a welcome option.

ARTIFICIAL, NON-CALORIC SWEETENERS

The use of aspartame, saccharin, and other artificial sweeteners has been a major consumer trend in the United States and Europe for decades. These sugar substitutes are mostly manufactured using chemical processes and non-natural ingredients; some, like sorbitol and xylitol, can be found in nature, but are produced commercially using synthetic sources. Just as with coffee and colas, consumers may choose these as alternatives to sugar for their tea, but they should be avoided because they distort the flavor of the tea. Diabetics and those with health-driven reasons for reducing calories may have no other practical alternative than stevia.

PAIRING TEA WITH FOOD

In much of Asia, tea is still largely prepared for daily enjoyment, on its own and with meals. In Great Britain and much of Europe, tea—primarily black tea—is still served as part of traditional afternoon tea, high tea, and as an accompaniment for various snacks and desserts. Tea balances nicely with many types of food, from meats and salads to cookies and cheese.

The notion of pairing specific teas to specific foods is a relatively recent phenomena. It is so new that rules laid down by tea connoisseurs may be more rules of thumb than concrete guidelines.

Pairing is one of the most fun pastimes involving tea; it can be a delight for guests to be served not only good quality, properly brewed tea, but to enjoy it accompanied by foods that complement the beverage.

Compatibility is the goal when pairing tea and food; it's important to identify teas and foods that have similar traits. Boldness and intensity is one example, matching a sharp cheese and a strong black or green tea. Conversely, some people will pair opposites, such as a tray of delicate fruits served with a bright but mellow oolong, creating a counterbalance between each bite and sip.

In tea and food pairing, mouthfeel is a major element. Mouthfeel refers to how a liquid or solid feels on the tongue and palate. When foods and beverages are paired, the balance or contrast between the two contributes to the overall sensory impression.

If a food is rich in fat from milk, cream, or meat, tea can serve as a softener or cleanser, gently altering the impact between mouthfuls. A creamy cheese or a scallop sautéed in butter might be accentuated by a green oolong or a Chinese Dragonwell green tea; either will complement the fats, while the nuances of the tea accent each successive mouthful. Desserts such as sorbets, ice creams, iced cakes, and cookies are especially tasty when served with just the right tea. A strong black tea can moderate the sweetness.

Some cooks now incorporate tea directly as an ingredient in their food, and it is often desirable to serve the same tea with the dish using it as an ingredient. The smoky Chinese black tea Lapsang Souchong is a popular ingredient for salmon and beef recipes, where a smoked essence is desirable. Earl Grey pairs well with dessert. The classic Japanese genmai-cha (green tea with popped rice) is exceptionally enjoyable when drunk with simple rice, vegetable, tofu, and seaweed dishes. Flavored and scented teas need to be assessed a little more closely before serving them with food, to ensure they do not overpower the food with which they are matched.

TEA-PAIRING SUGGESTIONS

• White tea has ultra-subtle flavors, but when brewed strong, it can enhance brie cheese, delicate pastries, or baked dishes prepared with lighter sauces.

• Black teas, especially those from Ceylon and India, are superb when paired with many foods, including meat, bread, chocolate, and sweets.

• Green teas from Japan and some Chinese teas work best with lighter fare, such as seafood, citrus fruits, sweets, and baked goods.

• Oolong tea from Taiwan works delightfully with just about everything.

PALATE CLEANSERS

It is common in Asia and other parts of the tea world for a small bowl of raw unsalted almonds or cashews to be served when tasting and savoring fine teas. The nuts act as palate cleansers and provide an often-needed bit of food for those with sensitive or empty stomachs.

How To Make Tea

INTRODUCTION

Now that you have traveled through the basics of tea, it is time to learn the simple art of making tea. Using step-by-step methods, you will discover the primary methodologies for preparing and enjoying tea as is commonplace in many of the top tea-producing and tea-consuming nations.

Each tea-producing origin produces distinctly different styles of tea with endless flavor, color, and aroma variations. Every region has evolved its own unique styles of brewing tea. The most detailed explanations on how to brew tea using traditional methods still popular within China and Japan are provided here in the most detail as they cover the greatest diversity of tea-brewing practices and tea types of any nations. The tea-loving countries of India, Great Britain, and North America and some of their more popular brewing techniques are described as well.

It now comes down to a few basic guidelines for brewing and using tea-brewing tools to make tea precisely the way you will enjoy. Here you will find how much tea to use, steeping times, and serving accoutrements and condiments. With each new tea you acquire, the enjoyment of discovering exactly how you prefer it becomes the last step in the whole tea experience. Brew it strong or light, add in condiments or not, serve it piping hot or let it cool—the variations are almost infinite.

The various tea-preparation techniques in this chapter are a starting point in your forthcoming tea journey; your personal preferences will guide you further.

TEA IN CHINA

There many methods used to prepare Chinese tea. This makes sense, as China is the birthplace of tea and literally hundreds of tea types, styles, and variations are abundant throughout the country. While tea consumption in China dates back thousands of years, the first records of formal tea ceremonies date from the Tang dynasty circa 619–907 CE. Ceremonies during these times were intricate, involving dozens of specialized brewing and serving accoutrements, accompanied by complex preparation rituals. It was not until 400 years later, however, that tea drinking became more commonplace at all levels of society, and undertaken with less pomp and ceremony.

GONGFU CHA TECHNIQUE

In more recent history, one popular practice for brewing Chinese teas using slightly modernized techniques is called Gongfu Cha. These brewing practices arose during the Ming dynasty with an occasional modification over subsequent centuries. Gongfu Cha means literally "making tea with effort." It can also be a relatively simple preparation technique, but its many nuances and variables require years of patient practice before one may claim any form of mastery; however, newcomers can enjoy it as well. This technique is now becoming popular in North America, Great Britain, and Europe, where it is embraced by specialty tea enthusiasts.

Gongfu Cha focuses heavily on tea quality: the perfect synergy of aroma, color, flavor, and even the shape of the leaves are sought-after goals. Many of the quality specialty teas grown in China have been processed specifically for Gongfu Cha–style brewing. These types of tea include strong black and heavily oxidized oolong teas. The brewing method described on page 128 can accommodate almost any type of tea, including black, white, and green teas.

A classic Gongfu Cha tea brewing
set on a wooden tea platform or "boat."

The wooden tea platform or "boat" is an indispensable part of the accoutrements needed for the Gongfu Cha method. This platform catches the drips and excess water that will flow when the teapot and tasting cups are warmed. It keeps the other surfaces free of excess water. Ensure you have a towel on hand to mop up any spills. Keeping the tea area orderly enhances the soothing aspect of the ceremony.

An important part of the tea ceremony is to take the time to inhale the volatile tea essences that condense inside the tall aroma cup. These scents will then evaporate slowly. Once the aromas have been appreciated, it is time to slowly sip and enjoy the tea.

Once the first serving has been completed, the entire process of infusing the tea with water can be repeated many times until the server feels the tea leaves are spent and will simply not produce another adequate infusion. Each successive steeping is a sensory journey as the tea slowly reveals its special aromas, flavor, color, and mouthfeel.

GAIWAN TECHNIQUE

Sometimes a more Western-style teapot made from either earthenware or ceramic, and larger than traditional Chinese vessels is used to brew Chinese tea. However, using a gaiwan teacup to brew and serve tea is a common Chinese method. Gaiwan—or *zhong*, as it is called in everyday use within China—means "covered bowl." Clay earthenware conducts heat extremely efficiently, therefore it is preferred for black tea preparation that requires very hot water temperatures. However, the gaiwan made from fine porcelain, or sometimes glass, is often used for the more sensitive and mellower green, white, and oolong teas that do not need to be overheated.

A gaiwan has dual uses, both as a small tea-brewing vessel and also as an individual teacup. It has no handle and is a simple, small bowl with a lid and a saucer. In the method on page 130, we have used a Chinese green tea, but as suggested above you can also experiment using white and oolong teas.

When you use a gaiwan to make tea, you can reuse the tea leaves by pouring more hot water over the previously brewed leaves and letting them steep again. Steeping times are generally slightly longer with each successive brewing as the leaves have given up some of their flavoring and aroma in the previous infusions. Some Chinese high-grade tea leaves will produce quite enjoyable brewed tea for at least five and even as many as ten steepings. You should experiment with each new batch of tea to determine the optimal steeping time for that specific tea, as this can vary from tea type to tea type, as well as the same type of tea that has been harvested in different seasons or different years.

It is desirable to use an unglazed, earthenware teapot or gaiwan exclusively for one type of tea. This avoids cross-contamination from aromas and over time, nicely seasons each pot.

A Chinese gaiwan that has an earthenware
exterior and a ceramic interior.

Part of the ritual of the tea ceremony is keeping the area neat and tidy so that you drink the tea in a soothing and relaxed atmosphere. It is customary to use a towel to wipe up spills and drips when brewing, keeping the tea boat and surrounding area dry and orderly.

When cleaning up, use tongs to remove all tea leaves from the gaiwan or teapot before rinsing, drying, and storing it. Always rinse the gaiwan or teapot with warm water and air dry between uses, and never allow soap or detergent to come in contact with it.

BREWING GONGFU CHA STYLE

Gongfu Cha is conducive to brewing heavily oxidized oolong teas. In this example, a dark Chinese oolong tea is used.

YOU WILL NEED

Kettle, Gongfu Cha teapot, reserve pot, tea boat platform, scoop, towel, aroma cup, tasting cups, water, oolong tea

METHOD

1 Place the Gongfu Cha teapot on the wooden tea platform (to catch the excess water) and pour boiling water over and into the teapot and cups, to warm them. Discard this water.

2 Use the scoop to measure the oolong tea into the teapot, fill it to about one-third of the volume of the pot (about 7 to 10 grams). An average Gongfu Cha teapot holds about 4 fluid ounces of water (approximately 120 ml).

3 Fill the teapot with hot water at 185 to 190°F (85 to 88°C), let it steep for 5 to 15 seconds, then pour it out. This procedure opens up the leaves and readies them for the main steeping.

4 Dry the outside of the teapot with the towel.

5 Refill the teapot with water (the same temperature as in step 3) and pour it just to the point of overflowing. Any froth or bubbles may spill out of the teapot and onto the tea boat platform.

6 Let the first infusion steep for about 30 seconds.

7 Drain the brewed tea into the reserve pot.

8 Pour some of this brewed tea "liquor" into the tall aroma cup.

9 Transfer the tea from the aroma cup into the tasting cups. Smell the aromas from the empty aroma cup before sipping the tea.

GONGFU CHA METHOD

STEP 1

STEP 2

STEP 7

STEP 8

BREWING TEA WITH A GAIWAN

Green teas are typically brewed using ceramic gaiwans. In this example, a Chinese green tea is used.

YOU WILL NEED
Kettle, gaiwan with a lid, towel, scoop, tasting cups, water, Chinese green tea

METHOD

1 Ensure the small teacups are placed directly next to the gaiwan, ready to receive the tea. A gaiwan holds from 5 to 7 fluid ounces (150 to 210 ml).

2 Pour heated water into the gaiwan that will be used as the brewing vessel. The water should be 160 to 185°F (71 to 85°C); the hotter the water, the stronger the brewed infusion.

3 Pour out this water after a few seconds, as this step is only done to warm the gaiwan prior to brewing.

4 Add the desired quantity of tea leaves to the gaiwan. Typically, this is a quarter to half of the volume of the gaiwan, or approximately 4 to 8 grams of leaves.

5 Pour the hot water (the same temperature as in step 2) over the leaves until the gaiwan is filled, then place the lid on top. The lid should remain in place during the steeping period. Steeping times vary widely, from 30 seconds to a couple of minutes.

6 Pour the tea into the cup. Either use the lid to prevent the tea leaves from escaping, or set a small strainer over the cup to stop the leaves from entering the cup. Repeat for the other cups.

7 Serve the tea, sip slowly, and savor the flavor.

GAIWAN METHOD

STEP 2

STEP 4

STEP 5

STEP 6

TEA IN GREAT BRITAIN

Tea first became popular in Great Britain during the seventeenth century when it was sold in England through London coffee houses. It was also sold in loose form, and soon women started to brew it at home. Hundreds of years later, it is the most popular beverage in Great Britain.

In Great Britain, using teabags is the most common way to make tea. However, as specialty teas become popular there is a return to brewing with loose tea. Traditionally, the British have drunk black teas including Assam, Ceylon, and Darjeeling. Although the method of tea-brewing described on page 134 is called "English," this type of tea is in fact drunk throughout Great Britain. The habit of adding cold milk to the tea is possibly one of the major differences between English tea and other brewing methods. There is always some discussion as to whether the milk should be added to the cup before the tea is poured in, or whether a dash of milk should be added after the tea has been poured into the teacup. Try both methods and see which you prefer. (For more information see page 117.)

Ceramic teapot

TEAPOTS

The classic English teapot is made from porcelain, a nonporous material. Unlike the earthenware used for many classic Asian teapots, porcelain teaware does not retain the scents and flavors of the teas brewed. It also heats much more evenly and somewhat more slowly than earthenware and therefore works for the more delicate green teas, although it is mainly the favorite of black-tea lovers in the West.

Silverware and stainless steel teapots were and are still used to brew and serve tea throughout Great Britain and Europe, but like all teapots, they have their limitations as well as advantages. A teapot made of silver will not chip or break. Conversely, silver and stainless steel may conduct heat so efficiently that they are not practical for green and some oolong teas, which are sensitive to high heat. For black teas that benefit from the intensity of heat, this type of teapot is most suitable.

Glass teapots are becoming more popular as they do not retain scent or flavors from each successive tea-brewing session, however, glass is quite fragile and can break easily. As glass is transparent you can observe the tea leaves as they release color and unfurl during the brewing process.

Stainless steel teapot

Glass teapot

BREWING ENGLISH TEA

English tea is often made with Assam, Kenyan, or Sri Lankan black teas, and cold milk is added to the cup.

YOU WILL NEED
Kettle, teapot, teacups, teaspoon, weighing machine, timer, tea strainer or infuser, water, loose black tea, milk, sugar (optional)

METHOD

1 Preheat the teapot by pouring in boiling water; let it sit for a minute, then discard the water. If you bypass this step, when the boiling water is added for steeping, it may cool by a few degrees from contact with the porcelain, reducing the effectiveness of the infusion stage.

2 Weigh the tea, approximately 2 grams of tea to 8 fluid ounces (240 ml) of water (or 1 teaspoon per cup). Put the tea leaves into the teapot (or into an infuser, and place that in the pot).

3 Pour boiling water over the tea leaves and replace the teapot lid.

4 Set a timer for the strength of tea desired. Start at 4 minutes, which is a common time for black teas brewed this way.

5 Gently stir the tea leaves a couple of times with a spoon. Replace the lid while it steeps.

6 Pour the brewed tea into individual cups; if you are not using an infuser, place a small strainer across the cup as you pour the tea.

7 Add milk to the cup either before the tea is poured or after, depending on your preference. If you wish, add sugar to taste.

ENGLISH TEA METHOD

STEP 1

STEP 2

STEP 4

STEP 6

ENGLISH TEA TIMES

Tea is the most popular beverage in Great Britain. Listed below are some of the ritual tea breaks that were taken historically. Some may still occur today in some form or other.

BREAKFAST In Britain tea is nearly always served at breakfast, although there will be an option for coffee. However, most people still like a cup of tea with milk in the morning.

ELEVENSES Elevenses is the equivalent of the American mid-morning coffee break. This tea occasion may be accompanied by a cookie (biscuit), or sometimes a croissant or a slice of cake. Brisk black breakfast teas are often drunk during these breaks.

AFTERNOON TEA Afternoon tea is traditionally served mid-afternoon, around 4 PM. It might just consist of a cup of tea, but it could also include a variety of sandwiches, cookies, and cakes.

CREAM TEA Cream teas are usually served in the afternoon. Traditionally, they originated in Devon in southwest England. Many rural parts of England (particularly Cornwall) now also serve cream teas. This consists of tea served with scones, clotted cream, and jam, usually strawberry, although other flavors may be available.

HIGH TEA High tea is served later in the day than afternoon tea, often around 6 PM. It is a relatively hearty meal that can be served with cheese, cold meat, meat pie or even sausage, fresh breads, and some type of dessert as well as tea. You may still find it served in Scotland and parts of northern England.

CELEBRATION TEAS Many hotels and upmarket tea salons worldwide serve teas for special occasions, usually in the afternoon. These might include a choice of special teas, fancy desserts, and even champagne.

TEA IN INDIA

Large-scale commercial production of tea in India began in the nineteenth century and the country remains one of the largest tea producers in the world. Drinking tea is extremely popular in India and 70 percent of India's annual tea production is consumed within the nation. India primarily produces black tea. Among many others, these popular teas include: Assam, the foundation of many breakfast teas; Darjeeling, the wonderfully complex "Champagne of Teas"; and Nilgiri, the mellow, high mountain tea of southern India.

Indian black teas may be enjoyed with or without the addition of milk or sweeteners, the exception being Darjeeling tea, which is quite delicate and complex, and therefore condiments are rarely added. Conversely, Assam black tea is quite brisk and bold and therefore some people add a dash of milk or sugar to soften the astringency a bit. Nilgiri is perfectly in the middle, delightful with or without condiments.

Tea is enjoyed in all strata of society within India and while some Indians still enjoy their daily tea prepared in the classic English manner using a ceramic teapot, many prefer chai—a delicious mixture of black tea and spices such as ginger, black pepper, and cardamom, with sugar and milk sometimes added. Roving tea sellers called "chai-wallah" offer freshly brewed chai on the streets, on trains, and in many businesses. The highly sweetened American chai drinks have little resemblance to classic Indian chai.

More than 150 years since its inception, Indian tea culture is changing rapidly. Until recently, green tea was unavailable; however, a tiny amount is now produced within India, and it's become the hip new beverage in upscale hotel lounges, tea bars, and quaint cafés. Multi-unit tea shops with contemporary tea bars are opening in the bigger cities, offering teas from all over the world.

BREWING INDIAN SPICED CHAI

This recipe for chai tea serves four people. You could use either tea bags or loose tea; Assam is used here.

YOU WILL NEED

Saucepan (stainless steel or glass, not aluminum), strainer, 4 mugs, milk frother (optional)

INGREDIENTS

3 cups milk (24 fl oz/710 ml) • 1 cup water (8 fl oz/240 ml) • 2 small cinnamon sticks • 2–3 whole cloves • 1 teaspoon cardamom pods • ½ teaspoon ginger powder (or 2 thin slices fresh ginger) • ¼ cup black tea (or 3 black tea bags) • ¼ cup sugar (or honey may be substituted) • 1 teaspoon vanilla (or 1 vanilla pod) • nutmeg powder for sprinkling

METHOD

1 Add the milk and water to a saucepan and heat over a medium-high heat until it starts to boil, then turn the heat down.

2 Place all the other ingredients into the mixture and let it simmer gently on a low heat for another 4 to 6 minutes (a longer time on the stove brings out the tea and spice flavors).

3 Remove the saucepan from the stove.

4 Place the strainer over each mug and pour the chai tea into the mugs one at a time, to remove the spices and tea.

5 Use a small milk frother to create foam on top of the chai tea. Position the milk frother near the top of the mug rather than submerging it in the milk.

6 Sprinkle a little nutmeg on top of the chai in the mugs and serve.

CHAI TEA METHOD

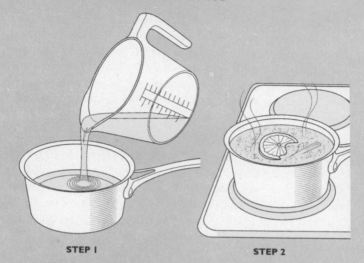

STEP 1

STEP 2

STEP 4

STEP 5

TEA IN JAPAN

Tea was consumed in Japan as early as the eighth century, but it was not until the twelfth century that a Buddhist monk named Eisai, returning home from China, carried seeds of the tea plant to Japan, where they were planted in the Uji region. Eisai is considered the founding father of the Japanese tea industry, as he also brought back from China the practice of grinding tea to a fine powder, which is called matcha tea.

Tea drinking in Japan is a unique hybrid of daily lifestyle and aesthetics— at least for some—and the ethereal realms of philosophy and religion. Much of this is embodied within the Japanese tea ceremony, called *Cha No Yu*, which literally means "hot water for tea." The ceremony is essentially a cultish practice teaching chado, or "the way of tea." *Cha No Yu* is focused upon finding and appreciating beauty in simple daily activities, particularly the enjoyment of tea.

MATCHA TEA

Matcha green tea has been the centerpiece tea of the *Cha No Yu* tradition for centuries, and in more modern times this prized Japanese powder has achieved international cult status among tea lovers. Matcha is made from nutrient-dense Japanese tea leaves that are shaded for a few weeks before harvesting, concentrating maximum levels of chlorophyll and certain nutrients, while simultaneously reducing bitterness. After harvest, the leaves are gently dried and ground into a fine powder.

Matcha is sold in many grades. Ceremonial grade is the highest quality and the priciest. All matcha should be a bright, almost phosphorescent green, sometimes described as jade.

Serve matcha with a simple snack such as butter cookies, unsalted almonds, or cashews. It is a potent tea that both fills the stomach and cleanses the palate.

A contemporary tetsubin teapot with a
metal infuser basket. This teapot is made of cast iron
with an enamel coating on the inside.

TETSUBIN TEAPOT

Cast-iron teapots originated in Japan, where green tea is favored, but
they also do a marvelous job of steeping hearty black teas, which stand
up to heat well.

The modern tetsubin teapot is made of cast iron with an enamel
coating on the inside. Cast iron conducts heat extremely efficiently and
will stay warm without a tea cozy. This ability to keep the teapot and
brewed tea inside hot can pose a dilemma. Sensitive teas, including
many green and scented teas, will stay too warm and become a little
over-steeped and bitter. To control this unwanted effect, remove the
inner basket strainer once the tea has steeped long enough, or
otherwise strain the tea into a separate serving pitcher.

OTHER JAPANESE TEAS

In the nineteenth century, farmers in Japan made a monumental leap in tea production by improving the post-harvest processing of tea leaves through the use of steam and rolling of the leaves to produce the first Japanese green tea, called sencha. Sencha rapidly became a hit and is still the most popular tea in the country. Later in the nineteenth century, labor-intensive harvesting of tea leaves was mechanized, which accelerated production times and boosted exports as quantities of tea rose significantly.

Tea drinking and the cultivation of plants spread slowly within Japan; originally, only the highest stratum of society indulged in this relative luxury. Today, tea is an integral part of Japanese society at every level and it is served everywhere; the most common types are hojicha or bancha tea, and at home, sencha is also popular. As a luxury, the precious gyokuro green tea is served, and matcha with its historical roots in Zen philosophy.

Tea is so intrinsic to Japanese society and culture that Japanese tea is referred to as o cha—always green tea. Black tea (not produced in Japan) is ko cha, which also refers to oolong and scented teas; many Japanese have a fondness for certain black teas (Indian Darjeeling is one example) and Taiwanese teas (fancy oolong teas).

JAPANESE TEA TECHNIQUES

Japanese tea preparation is truly a middle path when it comes to steeping times. Japanese teas typically steep for 2 to 2½ minutes, whereas classic Chinese tea brewing may be limited to 45 seconds to 1½ minutes, while Western-style teas have longer steeping times of 3 to 5 minutes.

A kyusu tea set with a teapot,
ceramic cups, and a reserve pot.

For the more commonplace Japanese teas such as bancha, hojicha, and genmaicha, a single steeping or infusion is standard. The more-prized Japanese sencha and gyokuro teas are often steeped up to three times.

KYUSU

In contemporary Japan, a nifty teapot called a kyusu is often used to brew finer-quality green teas. It is made from either porcelain or glass, has a snugly fitting tea filter inside, and a handle protruding from the side. This handle is exceptionally handy when pouring tea. The kyusu has a small capacity, about 1 ½ cups (360 ml).

Small, white ceramic cups without handles are preferred for drinking, but any type of small cup may be used.

BREWING MATCHA TEA

Matcha powder is measured carefully into special bowls, where it is combined with hot water, then whisked into a froth and served in small cups. In North America, matcha is sometimes mixed with hot milk and sweeteners to create a matcha latte.

YOU WILL NEED

A bowl (*chashaku*—it should be unglazed on the inside to help the matcha dissolve more easily), fine-mesh strainer, bamboo whisk (*chasen*), bamboo tea scoop (sometimes referred to as a spatula), small tasting cups (ceramic is preferred), matcha powder

METHOD

1 Measure 1 ½ to 2 teaspoons of matcha or use a bamboo spatula (1.5 to 2 grams per serving).

2 Gently sift the matcha through the strainer and into the bowl. This keeps the powder from forming lumps.

3 Pour ½ cup of water (120 ml), boiled and then cooled for a few minutes to around 165 to 175°F (74° to 79°C), over the powder in the bowl.

4 Start whisking immediately, vigorously stroking the *chasen* back and forth across the bowl (but not in a circle).

5 When a nice foam head starts to emerge, whisk the very top inch of the tea brew intensely, further developing a green, frothy, bubbly head.

6 Pour the matcha into the cups and serve.

MATCHA METHOD

STEP I

STEP 2

STEP 4

STEP 6

BREWING JAPANESE GREEN TEA

The method described below uses a kyusu teapot and is suitable for green teas such as sencha, genmaicha, hojicha, and gyokuro. Japanese green teas are not served with condiments such as sugar or cream.

YOU WILL NEED
Kettle, kyusu teapot, infuser or bamboo strainer, teaspoon, tasting cups, water, green tea

METHOD

1 Place a well-rounded teaspoon (about 1.5 grams) of green tea into the teapot for each serving the teapot holds, one serving per person. An average kyusu teapot holds 12 fluid ounces (360 ml). A serving ranges between 5 to 8 fluid ounces (150 to 240 ml), depending upon cup capacity. Measure the capacity in advance with water.

2 Bring the water to a boil, then let it cool for a few minutes. The water temperature should be 175 to 180°F (79 to 82°C) for sencha and other Japanese green teas such as genmaicha and hojicha; for gyokuro tea use 150 to 160°F (65 to 71°C).

3 Pour the water over the tea in the pot.

4 Let the tea steep for 2½ minutes for the first infusion. The second and third infusions can steep for 3 minutes.

5 Pour the brewed tea directly into each cup, if your kyusu teapot has a built-in infuser screen to catch the tea leaves. If not, use a small bamboo strainer over each cup.

GREEN TEA METHOD

STEP 1

STEP 3

STEP 4

STEP 5

TEA IN NORTH AMERICA

In recent years a tea renaissance in Canada and the United States has produced a groundswell of appreciation for fine tea. Concurrently, many science-based studies on the connection between tea consumption and health have emerged. North America is now considered the launchpad for a global interest in specialty tea with hundreds of emerging tea brands, multi-unit retail tea chains, and a vibrant tea culture. Tea culture is sweeping the globe.

PYRAMID-SHAPED TEA BAGS

Perhaps nowhere on the planet are tea bags used so often to brew tea than within North America. In the 1990s pyramid-shaped tea bags became available and consumers fell in love with their novel shape, silky feel, and the ability to watch tea leaves unfurl and release their goodness into the cup. These bags also allow tea leaves to expand considerably more than traditional tea bags, vital for obtaining a better cup of tea out of a bag. They have become exceptionally popular in North America and Asia. See the method of how to brew tea using pyramid tea bags on pages 150 and 151.

ICED TEA

Iced tea has been enjoyed as a beverage since at least the mid-1800s in both the United States and Great Britain. Back then, it was called tea punch, and usually had an added ingredient: alcohol. During the World's Fair of 1904, in St. Louis, Richard Blechynden, a tea vendor, added ice to make his hot beverages more appealing in warm weather. Blechynden's inspiration is credited with launching the commercial era for iced tea. Iced tea currently represents more than 80 percent of all the tea consumed in the United States.

Round "Assam" glass press-type teapot.

PRESS-TYPE TEAPOTS

North Americans love shortcuts, especially when it comes to saving time preparing foods and beverages. The modern press-type teapots are design take-offs on brewing devices like the coffee "French Press," by essentially using the same basic concept. An internal brew basket is filled with tea and then a built-in plunger device is pushed down into the infuser, essentially stopping the brewing process; small perforated holes in the infuser only run 80 percent of its length, so when the plunger is lowered, no more water contacts the tea leaves. A second pot of tea can be made simply by adding more hot water and once again moving the internal plunger up and then down. However, brewing hot tea in traditional ceramic teapots is still more commonplace in North America.

BREWING WITH PYRAMID TEA BAGS

The pyramid-shaped tea bags are made out of either all synthetic or corn-derived materials (meaning they are often biodegradable). They can be used for making individual cups of tea or a pot of tea. The method for both of these is similar. Some pyramid tea bags may be used to brew a second cup of tea; each type and brand of tea is different so you must experiment.

YOU WILL NEED

Kettle, tea cup(s) and/or teapot, pyramid tea bag(s), water, milk or cream (optional), sugar (optional)

METHOD

1 Remove any outer protective wrapping from the tea bag.

2 Place 1 tea bag in a cup and add boiling water.

3 Steep according to the directions on the package. As a rule of thumb: 2 to 3 minutes for green tea, and 3 to 4 minutes for black tea.

4 Remove the tea bag, using a spoon, and gently squeeze the tea bag as it is pulled from the water in order to extract more liquid and flavor from the tea leaves.

5 If you are using black tea you may wish to add milk, cream, or sugar. Green tea is usually consumed without adding condiments.

6 When using tea bags to brew tea by the pot, immerse 1 tea bag for each 6 to 8 fluid ounces (180 to 240 ml) of hot water the teapot holds. It is fine to lift the teapot lid and dunk the tea bags a few times as agitating the leaves makes a stronger brew.

PYRAMID TEA BAG METHOD

STEP 2

STEP 3

STEP 4

STEP 6

BREWING ICED TEA

Black tea is traditionally used to brew iced tea, but blends of different teas are becoming commonplace. Mixtures of green and mint tea, iced Earl Grey, and oolong all produce delicious iced tea. You can add squeezes of lemon or orange, sprigs of mint, and sugar or honey to the iced tea.

Hot Brewing Method

YOU WILL NEED

Two large jugs (one with a lid), strainer, glasses, tea, hot water, sugar or honey (optional), ice cubes, slices of lemon or orange (optional), sprigs of mint (optional)

METHOD

1 Place the tea leaves into a large jug with a lid. Use 2 teaspoons of tea (about 3 grams) per 8 fluid ounces of water (240 ml).

2 Add hot water to the tea, and cover the jug with a lid. Let the mixture steep for 6 to 12 minutes, depending on how brisk you prefer the final product.

3 If desired, stir in 1 teaspoon of sugar (or honey to taste) for every two cups, about 16 fluid ounces (480 ml). Add the sugar or honey while the liquid is still warm, as they do not dissolve easily in cold liquids. Let the brew cool to room temperature.

4 Once the tea has cooled and the sugar dissolved (if used), strain the liquid from the tea leaves into a cold pitcher. You can either refrigerate the pitcher for a few hours and then add ice cubes, or you can add ice cubes and serve immediately.

5 Pour the iced tea into glasses, and serve with slices of lemon or orange, or a sprig of mint.

ICED TEA: HOT BREWING METHOD

STEP 1

STEP 2

STEP 3

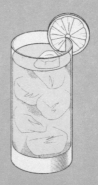

STEP 5

Cold Brewing Method

YOU WILL NEED

Two large jugs (one with a lid), strainer, glasses, tea, cold water, ice cubes, sugar (optional), slices of lemon or orange (optional), sprigs of mint (optional)

METHOD

1 Place the tea leaves into a large jug with a lid. Use 2 teaspoons of tea (about 3 grams) per 8 fluid ounces of water (240 ml).

2 Fill the jug with cold water either straight from the tap, filtered, or from a refrigerated source.

3 Put the lid on, place the jug into the refrigerator, and to improve the flavor and cool the tea, let it steep overnight.

4 After steeping, remove the jug from the refrigerator and strain the liquid from the tea leaves into another cold container. The resulting brew is typically smoother and mellower than the iced variety made from hot tea (see page 152).

5 If a sweetener is desired, vigorously stir in 1 teaspoon of sugar for every two cups, about 16 fluid ounces (480 ml) of brewed tea before serving. The tea is now ready to serve or it may be placed back in the refrigerator for storage. Typically, cold-brewed iced tea will stay fresh for up to 24 hours.

6 When serving iced tea, place ice cubes into tall glasses, pour over the tea, and garnish with slices of lemon or orange, or a small sprig of mint.

AFTERWORD

Tea has comforted and refreshed humans for thousands of years. From its ancient roots in China where it was first brewed in metal urns over open fires, to modern high-technology teapots, tea continues to satisfy our collective thirst with something few other prepared beverages deliver—a comforting, nutritious, and delicious pause to regroup and refresh.

For its first few thousand years of history, tea was made in the same manner with little significant variance from country to country. Boil water, drop a few tea leaves into a vessel of some kind, strain a few minutes later, and drink. It wasn't until the late twentieth century that creative entrepreneurs saw the potential of an awakening world tea marketplace, and clever new tea-brewing devices soon appeared. In the twenty-first century a stream of new teaware offering greater functionality and contemporary designs is being embraced by tea lovers everywhere.

Some are content to brew tea in the same ways favored by their ancestors, but a new generation of passionate tea aficionados is digging deeper to extract the sublime gems of ancient techniques, while inventing new methods and accoutrements. Tea culture is being reinvigorated to nurture modern needs for a tasty, affordable, and pleasurable product that can align with healthy lifestyles. Learning the basics of tea allows one to brew, serve, and sip this ubiquitous beverage in precisely the ways you like it: strong, mild, flavored, unflavored, sugared or unsweetened, hot or iced.

Thousands of new tea-centric cafés, shops, brands, and websites may pop up worldwide to serve all things tea, but you'll take great pleasure in knowing that you now know how to make tea.

Bibliography

Ahima, R. "Connecting Obesity, Aging and Diabetes." *Nature* 15 (2009): 996–7.

Barwick, Margaret. *Tropical and Subtropical Trees, An Encyclopedia.* Timber Press, 2004.

Brunning, Andy. Compound Interest. "Polyphenols and antioxidants—the chemistry of tea." www.compoundchem.com/2014/02/01/polyphenols-antioxidants-the-chemistry-of-tea.

Cannas, Antonello. "Tannins: Fascinating but Sometimes Dangerous Molecules." Cornell University College of Agriculture and Life Sciences. www.ansci.cornell.edu/plants/toxicagents/tannin.html.

Chin, Jenna, Michele Merves, Bruce Goldberger, Angela Sampson-Cone, and Edward Cone. "Caffeine Content of Brewed Teas." *Journal of Analytical Toxicology* 32 (2008): (8): 702–4.

Chow, Kit, and Ione Kramer. *All the Tea in China.* China Books, 1990.

Chung, K.T., Y.W. Huang, C.I. Wei, T.Y. Wong, and Y. Lin. "Tannins and Human Health: A Review." *Critical Review of Food Science Nutrition* 38 (1998) (6): 421–64.

Cook, Alexandra. "Linnaeus and Chinese Plants: A Test of the Linguistic Imperialism Theses." *Notes and Records of the Royal Society* 64 (2010).

Cummins, Joseph. *Ten Tea Parties: Patriotic Protest that History Forgot.* Quirk Books, 2012.

Deadman, Peter. "In Praise of Tea." *Journal of Chinese Medicine* 97 (2011): 14.

Delmas, Francois-Xavier. *The Tea Drinker's Handbook.* Abbeville Press, 2008.

Duke, James, A. "*Camellia sinensis* (L.) Kuntze." *Handbook of Energy Crops,* unpublished, 1983. www.hort.purdue.edu/newcrop/duke_energy/camellia_sinensis.html.

Emden, Lorenzo. "Decaffeination 101: Four Ways to Decaffeinate Coffee." *Coffee Confidential* (2014). www.coffeeconfidential.org/health/decaffeination.

European Food Safety Authority. "Scientific Opinion on the Substantiation of Health Claims Related to L-theanine from *Camellia sinensis* (L.) Kuntze (tea)." *EFSA Journal* 9 (2011): (6): 2238.

Goldender, Leonid. *History of Tea: Botanics.* Bouquet, 2003.

Hamilton, Dr. Susan. "November 2010 Plant of the Month—Tea Bush." University of Tennessee Institute of Agriculture. http://utgardens.tennessee.edu/pom/teacamellia.html.

Harler, Campbell R. "Tea Production." *Encyclopaedia Britannica* (2014). www.britannica.com/EBchecked/topic/585098/tea-production.

Harney, Michael. *The Harney & Sons Guide to Tea.* Penguin Press, 2008.

Hicks, Monique B., Peggy Hsieh, and Leonard N. Bell. "Tea Preparation and its Influence on Methylxanthine Concentration." *Food Research International* 29 (1996) (3–4): 325–330.

ITIS Standard Report Page: *Camellia sinensis.* Integrated Taxonomic Information System. www.itis.gov.

Lee, Chia-Pu, and Gow-Chin Yen. "Antioxidant Activity and Bioactive Compounds of Tea Seed Oil." *Journal of Agricultural and Food Chemistry* 54 (2006) (3): 779–784.

Lovell, Julia. *The Opium War.* Overlook Press, 2011.

Lowry, Nancy. "Tea and Theophylline." Amherst, MA: Hampshire College. http://helios.hampshire.edu/~nlNS/mompdfs/TeaTheoph.pdf.

Lu Yu. *The Classic of Tea.* Francis Ross Carpenter (translator). Ecco Press, 1995.

Meyer, Johann, Ludwig Roselius, and Karl Wimmer. "Preparation of coffee." (1908) U.S. patent 897840.

Mills, Ben, and Jenny Slaughter. "Tea (*Camellia sinensis*)." School of Chemistry, University of Bristol. July 30, 2014. https://chempics.wordpress.com/2014/07/30/tea-camellia-sinensis.

Mondal, Tapan. "Tea." *Biotechnology in Agriculture and Forestry*. Berlin: Springer; (2007): 519–520.

Moxham, Roy. *Tea: A History of Addiction, Exploitation, and Empire*. Carroll & Graf Publishers, 2003.

Neves, Marcos, Vinicius Trombin, Frederico Lopes, Rafael Kalaki, and Patricia Milan. "World Consumption of Beverages." Wageningen Academic Publishers (2012): 118.

Richardson, Lisa Boalt. *Modern Tea: A Fresh Look at an Ancient Beverage*. Chronicle Books, 2014.

Riley, Thomas. The University of Western Australia/Marshall Centre. "Tea Tree Oil." www.marshallcentre.uwa.edu.au/research/tea-tree-oil.

Schwalfenberg, Gerry, Stephen J. Genuis, and Ilia Rodushkin. "The Benefits and Risks of Consuming Brewed Tea: Beware of Toxic Element Contamination." *Journal of Toxicology* (2013); 370460.

Smith, William. *Dictionary of Greek and Roman Biography and Mythology*. Little, Brown and Co, 1867.

UK Tea & Infusions Association. "Tea growing and production." www.tea.co.uk/tea-growing-and-production.

USDA Database. "Oxygen Radical Absorbance Capacity (ORAC) of Selected Foods, Release 2 (2010)." www.ars.usda.gov/News/docs.htm?docid=15866.

van Wyk, B. *Food Plants of the World*. Timber Press, 2005.

Walcott, Susan M. "Brewing a New American Tea Industry." *Geographical Review* 102 (2012): 3, 350–63.

Resources

Rate Tea **www.ratetea.com**

Specialty Tea Institute **www.stitea.org**

Tea Association of Canada **www.tea.ca**

Tea Association of the USA **www.teausa.com**

Tea Biz Blog **www.teabizblog.wordpress.com**

Tea Chat **www.teachat.com**

The Daily Tea **www.thedailytea.com**

UK Tea & Infusions Association **www.tea.co.uk**

World Tea Academy **www.worldteaacademy.com**

World Tea Expo **www.worldteaexpo.com**

World Tea News **www.worldteanews.com**

Index

Acknowledgments

This book would not have happened without the many years of inspiring insights, education and inspiration of America's visionary tea scholar and author, James Norwood Pratt. Norwood's keen insights into the subtlest nuances of tea enjoyment and a passion for sharing the history of tea have simply been immeasurable. Many months ago the phone rang and it was Norwood calling to say we had to write this book for the millions of people who want a primer on the basics of brewing tea.

Additionally, we thank Mike Spillane, Mo Sardella, and Aaron Vick at The G.S. Haly Company, for their wealth of information—often on short notice—on the complex galaxy of specialty tea, from their insider's point of view.

Many thanks are also due to our many tea, beverage, and affiliated industry associates that were always available for a quick fact check, or referrals to other resources, as this book unfolded. And our hats are off to veteran food critic John Lehndorff, for always sending timely news on tea as well as general beverage trends.

And a very big thank you to our team at Ivy Press: editor Tom Kitch, copy editor Kate Duffy, illustrator John Woodcock, designer Ginny Zeal and art director James Lawrence. Their patient and supportive energy as this book unfolded has been exceptional. We hope they had the benefit of endless pots of steaming hot tea as the book developed.

Image Credits